BRUSSELS

KU-110-281

APA PUBLICATIONS

Part of the Langenscheidt Publishing Group

L

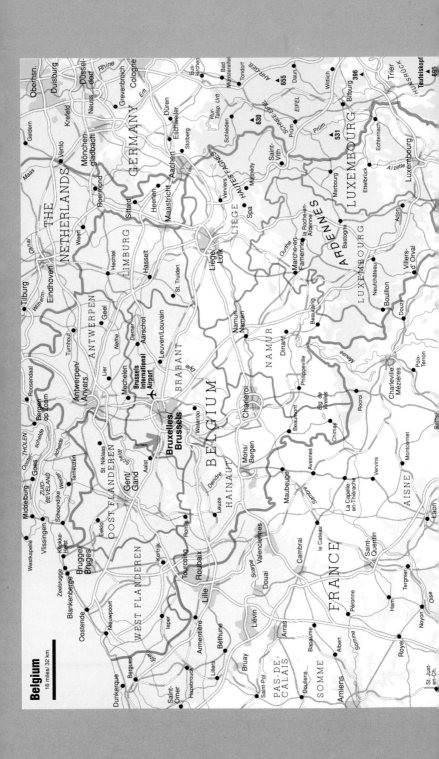

Belgium

16 miles/32 km

Welcome!

In my student days I used to go to Brussels for weekends — it was little more than across the street from where I lived in Germany. In those days I used to dream of exploring a world without boundaries; now, 25 years later, Brussels is busy creating the frontierless world that once existed only in my dreams.

In these pages Insight's correspondent in Brussels, George McDonald, has designed **15** itineraries to show you the best of Brussels. He begins with three full-day tours, the first exploring the area around the magnificent Grand'Place, the second following the historic Royal Road which cuts through the centre of the city, and the third focusing on the Bruparck and the Atomium. These are followed by **10** shorter itineraries, in which he takes you to some of his own favourite corners of the city, and two excursions, the first to Bruges and the second to Spa. In addition, there are sections on history and culture, eating out, shopping and nightlife plus a detailed practical information section.

 George McDonald is a journalist living and working in Brussels. In preparing this book his aim has been to get behind the 'Capital of Europe' tag and take you to the real city, where 'quality of life is the religion, superb cooking is taken for granted and conviviality is the only rule of the house in its many fine bars.'

C O N T E N T S

Pages 2/3:
flower carpet in
the Grand'Place

Excursions

Two interesting destinations within easy reach of Brussels.

Shopping, Dining & Nightlife

Calendar of Events

Practical Information

Maps

HISTORY &

Capital of Europe

Brussels, a city with a great deal of past, seems set for a bright future. As the developing 'capital of Europe', it can look forward to playing the role of Europe's Washington DC, the place where decisions affecting the lives of millions will be taken: one of the world's centre-stages of political power.

In some ways it is a strange choice for the role. Less cosmopolitan than Paris, less historic than Rome, less financially dominating than London, less emblematic than Berlin, Brussels is perhaps the ideal compromise. Not so long ago it was just the capital city of a small country, maybe a little bit sleepy, on the dividing line between Germanic northern Europe and the Latin south. Now it is on the fast track to global prominence and is changing rapidly as a result.

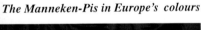

The Manneken-Pis in Europe's colours

What does it all mean? The strange thing is, officially, nothing. There's no such thing as a capital of Europe, at least not yet. Brussels just happens to be headquarters of the European Commission – which is like saying the District of Columbia just happens to contain the city of Washington. It also has a shiny new building that, by a strange coincidence, is perfect for housing a parliament, so that if the *European* Parliament should decide to settle down in a permanent home, Brussels can cough

Culture

modestly and point it out. Of course, that would be over the dead bodies of Strasbourg and Luxembourg, but dead bodies are no strangers to European history.

Brussels, like it or not, is a city of government – maybe more government than is good for it. There are politicians, civil servants, diplomats, lobbyists, pressure groups, and, yes, journalists, all labouring away in their various ivory towers on behalf of, or because of, the European Union, NATO, and the many and marvellous forms of Belgian government.

An Ancient Seat

Brussels is no newcomer to European power. Empires held court here before going with the turning world into history. In 1430, the felicitously named Philip the Good took possession of the Duchy of Brabant, of which Brussels was capital. Philip was Duke of Burgundy and although his official seat was in far-off Dijon, he was as keen as mustard on Brussels, which in effect became capital of Philip's empire-sized duchy.

The Burgundians brought with them a tradition of good living that has become proverbial: almost any newspaper or magazine article about Brussels contains a passing reference to the city's enviable 'Burgundian lifestyle'.

But a real empire was waiting in the wings. By the early years of the 16th century, the Habsburgs had absorbed Burgundy and

Philip the Good

The Ommegang

Brabant, and the Emperor Charles V set up shop in Brussels in 1515. Today, Charles's reign is evoked by a dazzling annual event that brings the 16th century to life in the Grand'Place. Called the *Ommegang*, it celebrates the procession organised to commemorate the emperor's return to his city in 1549. The *Ommegang* (from the Dutch for 'walk around') was even then a centuries-old tradition, originally held for religious reasons.

On the two evenings of the procession, held in the first week of July, only participants wearing 16th-century costume are allowed to take part in the performance in the Grand'Place. There are some 1,200 of them, many from old blue-blooded Belgian families, representing members of the imperial family and court, the aristocracy, magistrates, guildsmen, soldiers, militia and peasantry. Some, resplendent in red-black-and-yellow uniforms, parade on giant stilts, while others engage in elaborate displays of flag-waving and horsemanship. After dark, the ancient cobbled square turns into a witches' cauldron of coloured lights, dancing, music, fireworks and smoke.

The Habsburg Empire was actually a fairly late stab at a European Community, the Romans and Carolingians having trod this ground long before, but it was perhaps more recognisable as a community of nations. Emperor Charles lorded it over Germany, parts of Eastern Europe and Italy, as well as the Low Countries and Spain. In so doing, although his own reign was amiable enough, he stored up trouble for Brussels at the hands of less tolerant successors. When Philip II succeeded to the throne he clamped down hard on freedom of any sort, and Brussels rose against him. This proved to be a major miscalculation. Philip was big and mean; Brussels small and vulnerable. The price of revolt was the Holy Inquisition, executions and destruction.

Worse was to come. In 1695, Maréchal de Villeroy, commanding the army of France's Louis XIV – the 'Sun King' – in the Low Countries, needed a diversion from some siege or other. He found it by lining up his artillery hub-to-hub on the hills near Anderlecht and blasting Brussels' Grand'Place. The French gunners destroyed the medieval square, all except the Town Hall, in an act that Napoleon Bonaparte – himself no stranger to cannonades – said was 'as barbaric as it was useless'.

Napoleon was the next big name on the Brussels scene. During the French Empire, Brussels, along with The Hague, was one of the capitals of the occupied Kingdom of the Netherlands. Europeans have always found Belgium a congenial location for settling their quarrels and the 19th century was no different in that regard. The undulating fields south of Brussels, near the now famous village of Waterloo, saw the climactic denouement of the Napoleonic drama in 1815, when an Allied army routed the *Grande Armée* and sent the 'little corporal' packing.

In the settlement that followed this epoch-ending battle, Belgium was handed lock, stock and barrel to the Netherlands, but not for long. During a performance of the opera *La Muette de Portici* in 1830 at Brussels' Théâtre Royal de la Monnaie, one particular singer launched vigorously into an aria that spoke of freedom and love of country. It was an appropriately cultural way to start the patriotic revolution which instantly erupted, abolishing the short-lived Dutch rule and establishing Belgium's independence under Léopold of Saxe-Coburg, who was offered, and accepted, the position of King of the Belgians.

A State of Independence

The Belgians had their own country at last and could make either a good job or a hash of it as they saw fit. In fact, little Belgium became something of a wonder to the rest of Europe. Fired by the taste of freedom – as might be expected after waiting nearly a thousand years – the nation went straight to the forefront of the 19th century, when the application of science and engineering seemed to promise a vista of endless progress.

Belgium established continental Europe's first passenger railway, between Brussels and Mechelen. A wave of construction, in the grand style appropriate to a vibrant new nation, hit the capital. Among the edifying edifices was the Galeries Royales Saint-Hubert, Europe's first covered shopping arcade; the great triumphal arch and museum complex of the Cinquantenaire; and the Palais de Justice, whose way-over-the-top design renders even superlatives deficient.

That Belgium didn't live happily ever after is plain from the two German occupations of the 20th century. The country's biggest

The Belgian revolt of 1830

contemporary danger now comes from within: from the tensions between its Flemish and Walloon halves, with Brussels in the middle alternately claimed, courted and reviled by both. (There is also a small German-speaking community in the east, who claim, not without a touch of irony, to be the best Belgians of all.)

Extremists, or less pejoratively, enthusiasts, on both sides look forward to the day of division, but rumours of Belgium's demise have been touted before and have always proved greatly exaggerated. On the positive side, Belgium's painstaking construction of a *modus vivendi* between the two communities could prove a useful model for other European nations which are celebrating their new-found freedom by tearing themselves apart.

The Good Life

For the moment, Brussels is officially still only capital of Belgium, probably one of Europe's least appreciated countries. Non-Europeans often have difficulty even locating it on the map, yet it has an enviable tradition of good living and fine food, and few of the delusions of grandeur that have caused so much trouble in other countries over the centuries. That Belgians are not just *bons vivants*, however, is shown by the fact that the country is the EU's biggest exporter when judged per capita.

Unlike its bigger neighbours, Belgium does not trumpet its better tunes to the world. Such reticence may be due to the historical fact that whenever those neighbours *did* notice Belgium they decided they wanted it for themselves. Or it may be the natural reluctance of people who are in on a special secret to divulge the slightest hint of it, however much they may be tempted.

As Brussels' international clout grows, politicians, diplomats, business-people and tourists are discovering more of the good points of the city and the country. And Brussels is building an appropriate infrastructure. A new high-tech airport, fit to be the gateway to Europe's capital, has superseded the quaint old airport at Zaventem to handle the rapidly increasing number of arrivals. The TGV high-speed train network and the Eurostar from London have reached the city, and business investment is booming thanks to its role as capital of Europe and location at the transport nexus of western Europe.

Anyone who has spent time in Belgium will know that fine cuisine is one of life's priorities. Brussels has more Michelin-starred restaurants per head — or per stomach — than Paris,

Excellent food is the norm in Brussels

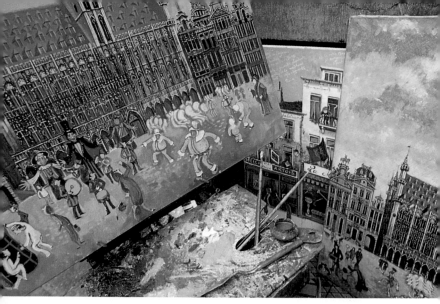

Contemporary paintings of the Grand'Place

yet even humbler establishments are rarely disappointing. Eating out is the big pastime of Brussels. The city is not especially notable for its nightlife or its theatre (although both do exist), but the food is something else.

Although it may have no cultural treasure-houses with the international allure of the Louvre, the Hermitage or the British Museum, there are more than 60 museums in the city, ranging from the artistically and historically significant to the downright surprising. The Musée d'Art Ancien displays a fine collection that includes works by Belgian Old Masters such as Brueghel and Rubens, while the underground galleries of the Musée d'Art Moderne are lined with the finest of contemporary classics: Magritte, Permeke, Ensor, and many others.

Belgium's Queen Paola

The Bruparck recreation complex in the northern suburbs has built on the success of the nearby Palais des Expositions, famed for the fabulously futuristic structure (even if it is nearly four decades old) called the Atomium. This symbol of Brussels, built for the 1958 World Expo, has loomed over the city ever since. Nine enormous spheres linked by tubular rods represent the atomic structure of iron, and look like an alien spaceship – landed, perhaps, to enquire about the possibility of an EU research grant.

Brussels is busily promoting itself as the Gateway to Europe, one effect of which is to draw attention to the city's location. London, Paris, Amsterdam and Cologne are all within easy reach. But

The Atomium, built for the 1958 World Expo

it would be a mistake to come to Brussels and ignore Belgium. Bruges would be placed among the front-runners in any league table of Europe's most beautiful cities, and Ghent would not be far behind. Antwerp, too, adds a vigorously Burgundian lifestyle to its more familiar role as Europe's largest port. Rugged hills and forests give the Ardennes region scenic splendour to accompany its renowned cuisine.

A veritable sea of green, Brussels boasts a number and extent of parks that would honour a city with many times its 1 million population. From the Bois de la Cambre in the south to the Parc de Laeken in the north, and at many points in between, Brussels offers its citizens most of the benefits associated – at least by city dwellers – with living in the country: fresh air, relaxation and a place of escape. Pride of place goes to the huge Forêt de Soignes, more like the tangled Ardennes forests than a park, which is remarkably untouched nature right on the city's doorstep and a favourite place for weekend walks.

Meanwhile, people who just want Brussels to continue being Brussels and long to get on with living in a city where quality of life takes the place of religion, see the ground-rules changing inexorably. Rents go up, districts change their familiar ways, the old certainties of life disappear. Brussels is destined to be the engine room powering a new force in the world, and the thrust is almost certainly unstoppable.

While there remains a surprising array of historic buildings in the city, Brussels has been cavalier with its architectural heritage, displaying an astonishing willingness to demolish *art nouveau* or *belle epoque* gems in favour of office blocks – but in that it's perhaps no different from many other cities where ignorance and profit walk hand in hand. There are signs that attitudes are changing, however. A veritable blizzard of restoration is underway and pressure groups keep a watchful eye on the developers.

Historical Outline

AD712 The Bishop of Cambrai dies in what will later become known as Brussels.

966 The first documented reference to Brussels, then called 'Bruocsella'.

977 A castle, or *castrum*, is built on the island of Saint-Géry.

979 The Duke of Lotharingia, son of the French king, occupies the castle. Traditionally, this is the city's founding date.

1100 Around this time the first defensive wall of Brussels is built.

1225 Construction of the Cathédral Saint-Michel.

1402 Work begins on the Town Hall.

1430 Philip the Good, Duke of Burgundy, takes possession of Brussels, making it *de facto* capital of his realm.

1514 Vesalius is born in Brussels.

1515 The Habsburg Emperor Charles V occupies the Coudenberg Palace.

1521 Erasmus lives in Anderlecht, then a village outside Brussels.

1531 Brussels becomes capital of the Spanish Netherlands.

1555 Charles V abdicates.

1568 The counts of Egmont and Hornes are beheaded for for championing the people's liberties.

1569 The painter Pieter Brueghel the Elder dies in his home on Rue Haute.

1695 Bombardment and destruction of the Grand'Place by a French army.

1715 The Treaty of Utrecht cedes the Low Countries to Austria.

1789 The French Revolution. Brussels rises up against the Austrians.

1794 Belgium becomes part of France.

1803 Napoleon Bonaparte visits Brussels as the First Consul of the Republic.

1815 Napoleon defeated at Waterloo. Belgium is ceded to the Netherlands.

1830 The Belgian revolt and War of Independence.

1831 Léopold of Saxe-Coburg installed as first King of the Belgians.

1835 The first continental railway, from Brussels to Mechelen, is inaugurated.

1847 Europe's first shopping mall, the Galeries Saint-Hubert, opens.

1871 Construction of the grand boulevards through the marshy area of the lower city. The River Senne is covered over throughout its length.

1914–18 World War I. Brussels occupied by the Germans.

1935 World Exhibition at the Heysel Parc des Expositions.

1940–44 Brussels occupied by Nazi Germany during World War II.

1951 Baudoin, late King of the Belgians, ascends the throne.

1958 The World Fair at the Heysel. The Atomium opens.

1959 Brussels becomes headquarters of the European Community.

1967 NATO moves to Brussels from Paris.

1979 The city of Brussels celebrates its millennium.

1980 The 150th anniversary of Belgian independence.

1989 In the reorganisation of the Belgian state, Brussels becomes the Capital Region, alongside Flanders and Wallonia.

1993 King Baudoin dies. His brother, Prince Albert of Liège, takes the throne as King Albert II.

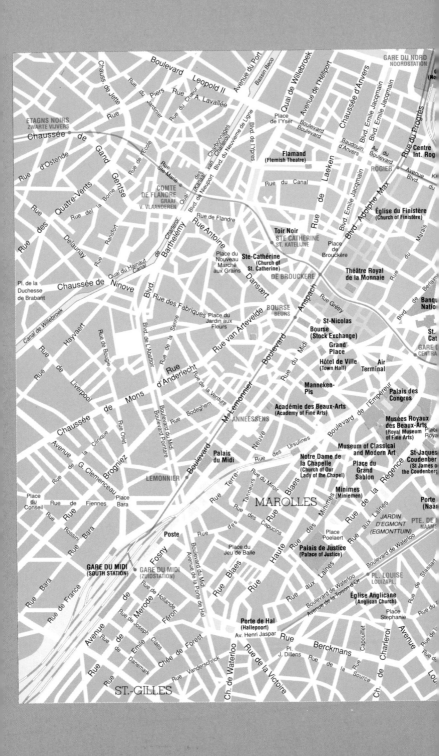

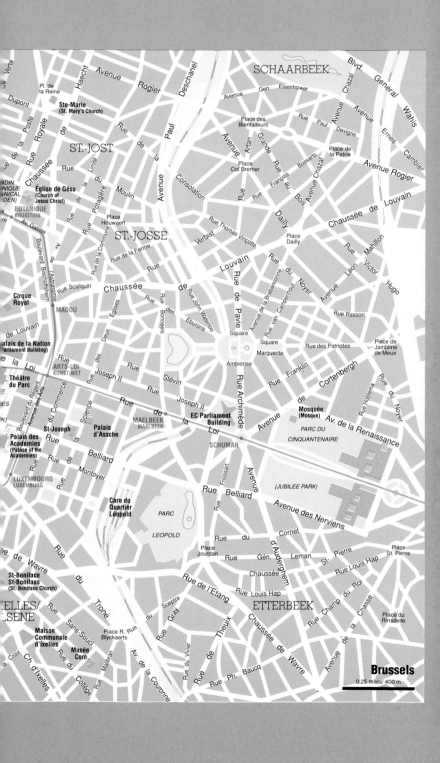

Brussels

0.25 miles/ 400 m

Brussels is a crossroads city, and a city at a crossroads. It sits smack on the dividing line between Germanic northern Europe and the Latin south – a geographical distinction the ancient Romans would have recognised, although Brussels didn't exist in their time. It is also coming to terms with its further internationalisation as *de facto* capital of Europe.

It is a bilingual city – French and Dutch – with English close behind. In this book I've chosen to give all place names in French, a decision the Dutch-speakers will hate. Few foreigners speak Dutch, although purists may be slightly mollified when I tell them that my Dutch is better than my French.

The city centre is shaped like a pentagon, or, more romantically, a heart, delineated in the past by the city walls and now by the inner ring road. Within that distinctive shape Brussels is in a state of flux, with construction, restoration, destruction and rebuilding going on at a frenetic pace. The first two day-long itineraries which follow give what I think is the essential introduction to Brussels, while the third covers the Heysel exhibition and Bruparck leisure complex, where many business visitors and tourists seem to end up. The itineraries are designed to be done on foot because Brussels is a relatively small – yet surprisingly tiring – city. Besides, the usually tranquil Bruxellois turn into red-eyed demons behind the wheel, as they negotiate the *priorité de droite* traffic system.

After this introduction, you can move in for a closer look with the half-day or evening itineraries.

I have two recommended day-trips. Belgium has a Flemish (Dutch-speaking) half and a Walloon (French-speaking) half and the day-trips reflect this. One is to the incomparable town of Bruges (Brugge) and the other to the originator of the thermal spa tradition, an Ardennes town called – what else? – Spa.

The Grand'Place

Start with the best approach to the Grand'Place, followed by a quick circuit of the guild-houses and a visit to the Musée de la Ville. Lunch, then homage to the Manneken-Pis en route to the Cathedral. To the Place des Martyrs via the comic strip museum, and finally a drink in the Hotel Metropole.

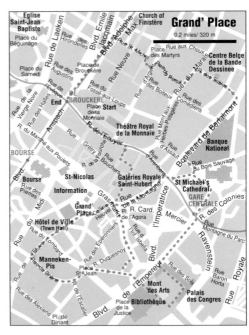

–Starting point is Place de la Monnaie, near the bus terminus and metro station at Place de Brouckère–

Your first day starts by the **Théâtre Royal de la Monnaie**, both opera house and ballet theatre. It makes a strikingly appropriate setting for its art thanks to a combination of dignity and exuberance imparted by the neo-classical design in dazzlingly white stone.

But don't linger here; go uphill on Rue de l'Ecuyer, right onto Rue des Dominicains then left

The Galeries Royales Saint-Hubert

into the **Galeries Royales Saint-Hubert**, Europe's first shopping mall, forerunner of other city arcades such as the Burlington in London. Designed in Italian neo-Renaissance style by architect Jean-Pierre Cluysenaer, the elegant triple-gallery – Galeries des Princes, Galerie du Roi and Galerie de la Reine – built between 1846 and 1847, has many fine shops, including the Ganterie Italienne glove-shop, Delvaux handbags and leather goods, and the Neuhaus *choco-laterie*. Here also is the excellent restaurant De l'Ogenblik, the café/terrace Mokafé, and the Taverne du Vaudeville, a bar and upmarket disco. The galleries are split by Rue des Bouchers, part of the restaurant-intensive **Ilot Sacré** (see The Ilot Sacré: Brussels à la Carte in the *Pick & Mix* section).

Emerge from the Galeries Royales Saint-Hubert and cross Rue Marché aux Herbes into Rue de la Colline: you're in for a surprise at the end. First-time visitors to the **Grand'Place** often stop in their tracks, gazing around in wonder as though the pearly gates had just opened in front of them. The ornamental gables, medieval banners and gilded facades might just be the mechanisms of a time machine, sweeping you back through the centuries to the days when powerful guilds and barons ruled Brussels.

This is the heart of Brussels. Its magnificent Flemish Renaissance-style buildings dating from the late 1690s were the headquarters of the great trading and mercantile guilds: tailors, butchers, brewers, bakers, cabinet-makers, haberdashers, boatmen, tallow merchants, and many others. The superb Gothic **Hôtel de Ville** or Town Hall seems to have something subtly wrong with it. The belfry is not only off-centre, it also has an off-centre entrance arch. Apparently it was all planned that way.

Cathédral Saint-Michel

The Grand'Place is the city's forum, especially in good weather when the terraces of cafés such as **Le Roy d'Espagne** and **La Chaloupe d'Or** are open. This is the place where visitors like to see and be seen. Beer is the business of the occupants of **La Maison des Brasseurs**, headquarters of the brewers' guild, and site of a museum (10am–5pm) devoted to the brewer's art. Belgium produces more than 400 kinds of beer and the museum's nominal entrance fee includes a chance to sample the finished product.

Most of the guilds no longer exist or have moved to humbler premises. The **Maison du Cygne**, once the butchers' guild-house, is now an exclusive restaurant, which is ironic because Karl Marx worked on *The Communist Manifesto* there during a three-year stay in Brussels. Across the square at **Le Pigeon**, now a Brussels-lace shop, penmanship of an equally radical kind aimed at Napoleon III earned Victor Hugo an invitation from the city fathers to leave town be-fore the outraged French emperor sent an army to collect him.

Earlier times are on display at the **Maison du Roi** (King's House). Inside, in the **Musée de la Ville de Bruxelles** (Monday–Thursday 10am–12.30pm, 1.30–5pm; weekends 10am–1pm; Oc-tober–March 1.30–4pm), you can trace the development of the city from a Dark Ages village to the Capital of Europe. In the exhibits are fascinating glimpses of a Venice-like town, clustered along the River Senne, which has long since been paved over. And there are the 400 or so costumes of Manneken-Pis, the symbol of Brussels, including army uni-forms, football strips and a skin-tight Elvis suit. More about this cheeky lit-tle statue below.

It's bound to be lunch-time by now, so why not try the traditional Belgian cooking in **'t Kelderke**, an atmospheric and convivial restaurant in the cellar below No 14.

The Manneken-Pis

Exit the Grand'Place on Rue Charles Buls which runs onto Rue de l'Etuve. And there he is, on the corner of Rue du Chêne, pid-dling away like crazy, more than likely confronted by a crowd act-ing as if they've never seen the likes before, which maybe they haven't. I'm talking about **Manneken-Pis**, the statue of a little boy doing what a little boy's gotta do, and doing it with all the glee-ful verve of any little boy who's ever taken part in a 'let's-see-who-can-pee-the-farthest competition'. The **Poechenellekelder** tavern opposite is worth a visit for its olde worlde charm and its collec-tion of theatre marionettes.

Carillon clock, Mont des Arts

Continue up Rue du Chêne — perhaps with a short sidestep on Rue Villers to see the **Tour Villers** and a section of the **city wall** — until **Place de la Vieille Halle aux Blés**, whose old Flemish houses have been getting some badly needed restoration. Come left to Place Saint-Jean, then onto Rue Saint-Jean and left through **Galerie Bortier**, notable for its old book and print shops. Go downhill on Rue de la Madeleine, past the Eglise de la Madeleine, to **Place de l'Agora**, where a sculpture of a 19th-century mayor of Brussels, Charles Buls, sits by the fountain, and which features a handicrafts market at weekends.

From here you climb Rue de la Montagne and cross Boulevard de l'Impératrice then up the stairway to the great **Cathédral Saint-Michel**. An alternative is to retrace your steps up Rue de la Madeleine and cross Boulevard de l'Empereur to the ornamental garden of the **Mont des Arts**. This street up to the cathedral also passes the wall-mounted **carillon clock** on the Mont des Arts, with 12 figures representing scenes from Brussels' history.

The cathedral is that curious mixture of cool silence interrupted by tour-guide chatter and clicking cameras familiar in all European cities. Construction began in the 13th century, the Early Gothic cathedral replacing an earlier Romanesque effort, and continued until the 17th, with additions right up to the present time.

Capturing Brussels on canvas

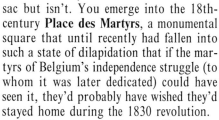

Its white stone exterior offsets the relatively plain interior, which nevertheless has some light touches – an altar supported by carved pelicans, and superb stained-glass windows.

Outside, return to Boulevard de l'Impératrice, or rather its continuation, Boulevard de Berlaimont, past the Banque Nationale, then cross over at the traffic lights and down the stairway to Rue des Sables. At No 20 is another kind of Brussels monument, the **Centre Belge de la Bande Dessinée** (Tuesday–Sunday 10am–6pm, closed Monday), otherwise known as the CÉBÉBÉDÉ.

This is the comic strip museum, housed in a magnificent *art nouveau* building by Victor Horta called the **Magasins Waucquez**, dating from 1903. Inside, there are collections and recollections from some of the greatest: Asterix, Lucky Luke, Thorgal and, of course, Belgium's own Tintin, created by the late Georges Remi, whose initials, when reversed and pronounced in French, give you *errjée,* or Hergé as he preferred.

After you've seen what you want here, turn left onto Rue du Marais then right onto Rue du Persil, which looks like a cul-de-

sac but isn't. You emerge into the 18th-century **Place des Martyrs**, a monumental square that until recently had fallen into such a state of dilapidation that if the martyrs of Belgium's independence struggle (to whom it was later dedicated) could have seen it, they'd probably have wished they'd stayed home during the 1830 revolution.

Crumbling masonry, broken pillars, shattered roofs, grass-grown cobbles, vandalised windows, busted fences, verdegris-covered lamp-posts and even bushes growing out of walls – as fine a state of dissolution as you could hope to see. Restoration is giving the city back its once-elegant square.

At the **Hotel Metropole** back at Place de Brouckère, the glittering French Renaissance-style foyer and the chandelier-encrusted, mirrored halls and public suites are a restful taste of the *belle epoque* in what is otherwise one of the city's most hurried districts. On no account should you miss a glass of something restorative in the café or on the street terrace.

Grand'Place facades

DAY 2

Palais de Justice

The Royal Road

This is a monumental itinerary (in more ways than one), but the all-day walk, starting about 9.30am, is divided by Brussels' main city-centre park and punctuated by café breaks.

–To starting point: bus 34 from De Brouck-ère station near Place de la Monnaie; journey takes about 10 minutes–

Get off the bus at **Place Louise** and come out onto Rue des Quatre Bras. Almost immediately you come to the **Palais de Justice** (Monday–Friday 9am–4pm) one of the biggest heaps of monumental stones in the country (perhaps in any country), dedicated to the awesome majesty of the law.

The palace's great double-sided staircase is guarded at one end by a statue of Cicero, looking suitably litigious despite a broken-off Roman nose, and of Ulpian, hefting a sword that looks mightier by far than a pen; at the other end you have Demosthenes and Lycurgus, far-seeing visionaries rendered in stone.

Beneath the binocular-lined esplanade on **Place Poelaert**, literally under the stern gaze of the law, is Brussels' iconoclastic working-class **Marolles** district (see *The Marolles: A Threatened Community* in the *Pick & Mix* section). In the middle of the square, named after Joseph Poelaert, the architect of the palace, is a bronze-and-stone monument to the Belgian Infantry that fought in World War I.

Take the road pointing away from the entrance to the Palais de Justice, Rue de la Régence, cross to the right side and continue

Outside the Eglise St Jacques sur Coudenberg

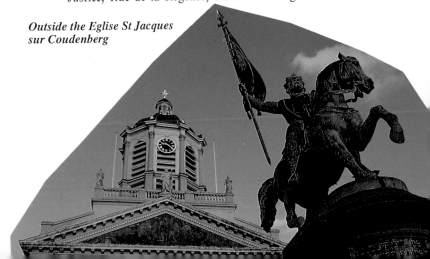

across Rue Joseph Dupont. On your right is Brussels' 180-year-old main **Synagogue**, which somehow managed to survive the war and which may be visited on weekdays when there is a service on, if you're quiet, discreet and don't take pictures. Next door, at No 30, is the **Conservatoire Royal de Musique**.

At the next corner is the **Musée Instrumental**, but because of opening times, I suggest you visit this and the surrounding **Grand Sablon** and **Petit Sablon** squares on another itinerary (see *The Sablon Squares* in the *Pick & Mix* section). The museum is due to relocate, however, and if it has done so when you read this, you can visit it later on this itinerary.

So, staying on Rue de la Régence, but crossing to the left side, within a minute or so you come to a small **Jardin de Sculpture** with a fountain, and benches where you can rest for a few minutes. Next is the palatial building which houses the **Musées Royaux des Beaux-Arts**, plural because there is the **Musée d'Art Ancien** (Tuesday to Sunday 10am–noon, 1–5pm, closed Monday) and the connected **Musée d'Art Moderne** (Tuesday to Sunday 10am–1pm, 2–5pm, closed Monday).

Hanging in the galleries of the ancient art museum, there is, as you might expect, a fine collection of works by Brussels resident Brueghel the elder, his son Brueghel the younger and Rubens. But there are also paintings by Van Gogh, Gauguin, Renoir, Jordaens, Ensor, Seurat, Rops, and many others.

It's all underground art in the modern art museum, at least in the sense that you have to go below ground level to

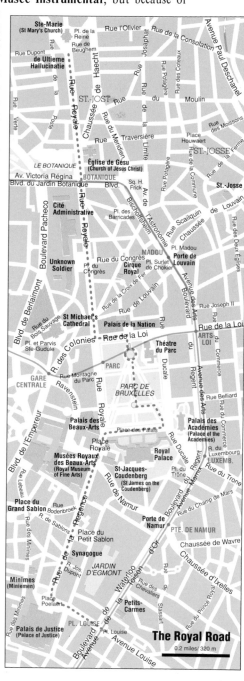

The Royal Road

0.2 miles/ 320 m

see it. There are eight floors on the descending tour. The trip is worth it when you can return with memories of Magritte, Dalí, Permeke, Dufy, Nam June Paik, Delvaux and a host of others.

Emerging from the museum and continuing on Rue de la Régence, take Rue du Musée on your left to a courtyard almost surrounded by the graceful museum complex, formerly the palace of the Duke of Lorraine, and a glimpse into the hemispherical hole in the ground where the modern part is located. An alleyway at the end takes you to **Coudenberg** and a fine view over the gardens of the Mont des Arts.

At No 68 Coudenberg is the **Taverne Le Coudenberg**, a simple Brussels tavern, for lunch. Afterwards go uphill to the magnificent, symmetrically laid-out **Place Royale**, surrounded by mansions in late 18th-century classical style. In the middle of the square is an equestrian statue of Godefroid de Bouillon, a crusader hero, first King of Jerusalem (surely arguable), who died in the Holy Land in the year 1100.

Also on Place Royale is the neo-classical **Eglise St Jacques sur Coudenberg** and on the opposite side a palazzo-style building that is eventually intended to house the Musée Instrumental, which may or may not yet have moved from its original location on the Petit Sablon. The square has recently undergone a process of badly-needed restoration, which has returned it to its rightful glory.

In the Musée d'Art Moderne

After Place Royale, the Rue de la Régence becomes **Rue Royale**, and the first place of interest on it, the **Palais des Beaux-Arts** (Tuesday to Sunday 10am–4.45pm, closed Monday), is at the beginning on the left. It hosts frequent visiting exhibitions and is also a venue for classical music concerts.

Directly across Rue Royale is **Place des Palais**, with the **Musée Bellevue** (10am–4.45pm), which has a fine collection of 18th and 19th-century *objets d'art*. Most of Place des Palais is occupied by the **Royal Palace** and its front gardens. King Albert has his office inside and it is used for state receptions. The royal family's main residence is out of town, however, near Laeken. Anyway, the guys with the neat uniforms and sharp bayonets won't let you in except during the period starting 21 July and lasting until some time around September.

Now it's time to cross over the square and rest under the shade of the trees. The **Parc de Bruxelles** was put there for that very purpose. Although not especially big, the French-style *jardin*, which

Rotunda in the Jardin Botanique

was formerly a royal hunting preserve, has been cleverly laid out, combining trails through the undergrowth with open avenues.

From the big fountain at its far end, beside Rue de la Loi, the central axis looks straight in the front door of the Royal Palace. Another main axis looks past old Godefroid all the way to the Palais de Justice, while the third looks out on nothing in particular — perhaps whatever was once there got demolished.

You should leave by the exit on Rue de la Loi, which is lined with yet another palace, the **Palais de la Nation**, although as this is occupied by the perenially squabbling Parliament, it ought perhaps to be demoted from the rank of palace. The armed forces keep an eye on the place and there are always lots of serious-looking soldiers outside — enough to make any politician nervous.

Back on Rue Royale again, cross over and walk for about 5 minutes until you reach the **Colonne du Congrès**, topped by a statue of Léopold I, with the Tomb of the Unknown Soldier and the eternal flame at its base. Behind the monument is an esplanade which gives a good view over the city skyline. Returning to Rue Royale, on the other side at No 13 is a surprising flower shop in *art nouveau*-style by Paul Hankar, **Les Fleurs Isabelle de Backer**, and at No 103 the magnificent **Hotel Pullman Astoria**, well worth a stop for a look round the *belle epoque* foyer and other public rooms, and a drink in the bar.

If you're wilting, you might want to call a halt to the day here. But there are a few more things to see

Refreshment in the Parc de Bruxelles

on Rue Royale. One is the **Jardin Botanique**, which used to be the Botanical Gardens. Now the beautiful glass-houses, dating from 1826, with their rotunda and gardens, are home to a French-community cultural centre, and there are regular events and exhibitions.

If you can bear with me a little further, to the café **De Ultieme Hallucinatie** at No 316, I don't think you'll regret spending the evening here. Inside, there's *art nouveau* design and fittings, a rock-face that looks fit for climbing and a patio with couches. The menu is excellent although not exactly cheap.

DAY 3

The Atomium and Mini-Europe

A day in the Bruparck, to a theme-park that's popular with tourists and that the Bruxellois, although maybe a little sheepishly, seem to be taking to their hearts.

–To starting point: metro 1A (direction Heysel) from De Brouckère station near Place de la Monnaie; journey takes about 20 minutes–

If you decide to go for the whole Bruparck experience, you'll need to bring swimwear. You should aim to be there about 11am and can stay until late afternoon or into the evening if you want. Entrance tickets for the various attractions are not cheap, but you can save money by buying a combination ticket. Should there be an interesting exhibition at the **Parc des Expositions** such as the car show, you might want to go earlier.

Most cities have an identifying symbol: Paris has the Eiffel Tower, London has Big Ben, New York the Statue of Liberty, that sort of thing. If they don't, they just build one, which is what Brussels did in 1958 for the World Expo hosted by the city. The result was the **Atomium** (open 1 April t o 31 August 9.30am–8pm; 1 September to 31 March 9.30am–6pm), as fabulous in its way as the Eiffel Tower and the Statue of Liberty, and just about as useless – at least Big Ben tells you the time.

Model of the Grand'Place in Mini-Europe

In any case, there it is, towering over you when you emerge from the **Heysel** metro station, halfway down Boulevard du Centenaire. It is built from nine spheres, great metallic ones joined by spars and tubes, that combine to represent the atomic structure of iron. It looks like a set straight out of *Star Wars*; all you need do is light the blue touchpaper, stand back and the next stop is Alpha Centauri. The reality is a little less romantic, but you should savour

The Parc des Expositions

Pool in the Océade

the impact of your first glimpse, because you'll never see anything quite like it again.

After the Expo the Atomium's owners must have spent a deal of time scratching their heads and asking themselves: 'Now what do we do with it?' What they did was put a science exhibition inside and a pretty good restaurant, **Chez Adrienne**, right on top.

The science is all about genetics and heredity and viruses and infections and AIDS and vaccinations and other such cheery subjects. Fascinating, but maybe not calculated to improve your appetite. Anyway you'll most likely need reservations for the restaurant. On the same floor – or more accurately in the same sphere – there's an observation deck with a superb view over Brussels.

Outside again, about halfway up Boulevard du Centenaire you cut across the car park on the left to the **Bruparck** entrance. Go upstairs and through the archway. Directly ahead is one of Brussels' institutions – the restaurant **Chez Léon**, a branch of the chain

Italy (left) and Spain represented in Mini-Europe

whose best-known outlet is in the city-centre Ilot Sacré (see *The Ilot Sacré: Brussels à la Carte* in the *Pick & Mix* section). This is the place for a light lunch, especially one of their *moules* (mussels) specialities. There are plenty of other restaurants to choose from if seafood doesn't appeal.

Afterwards, take the stairs inside the park past the marvellously old-fashioned double-deck magic-roundabout with wooden horses, to **Mini-Europe** (25 March to 30 June and 1 September to 1 November 9.30am–6pm; 1 July–31 August 9.30am–8pm; 2 November to 8 January 10am–6pm), which is just what its name suggests.

Some of the finest European architectural and engineering creations are presented with commendable realism in Mini-Europe, but at 1:25 scale. Each of the 15 European Union countries is represented. You can stroll around the Leaning Tower of Pisa, the Palace of Westminster, the Acropolis, the Arc de Triomphe, the canals of Amsterdam, the Brandenburg Gate, the Belfry in Bruges, and many others. It's fascinating, and if nothing else at least it saves the air fare to see the real thing. Don't be surprised if two hours slip past in Mini-Europe without you realising.

There is a good **Planetarium** beside the Heysel Football Stadium, just outside the park on Avenue de Bouchout, but it operates minimal and eccentric hours.

Next, however, you might want to go for a beach party in the **Océade** (open almost every day by 2pm, sometimes earlier). This is one of those aquatic paradise places with giant flumes, wave machines, palm trees, plastic beaches, poolside bars, etc. It's fun at any time, but for my money it's best on a freezing-cold winter's day, when you can pretend to be in the Bahamas.

Assuming that it's mid to late afternoon by now, you could al-

ways have a coffee or a beer in the **Village**, an Olde Brussels-style (but modern) bundle of shops, cafés and restaurants. And for a combination of passive entertainment and rest Bruparck also has the **Kinepolis**, which calls itself the biggest cinema complex in the world. There's bound be something worth seeing in its 29 theatres, where all films are shown in their original languages, and most are American. Kinepolis also has an IMAX theatre with a wrap-around screen that takes you on a realistic journey inside a volcano or across the icy wastes of Antarctica. Bruparck's that sort of place.

Morning Itineraries

1. The Sablon Squares

Atmosphere and charm in the Place du Grand Sablon and its smaller cousin, the Place du Petit Sablon. Antiques everywhere.

–To starting point: bus Nos 34, 95 or 96 from Rue Henri Maus beside the Bourse, or you can always walk from the Grand'Place, following the frequent signposts to the Grand Sablon–

The best time for this itinerary is at the weekend, when an open-air **antiques market** (Saturday 9am–6pm, Sunday 9am–2pm) takes place on **Place du Grand Sablon,** and especially a Sunday when the traffic is quieter. Even without the market these squares are pretty interesting. You may want to slip an extra few francs in your pocket because the Sablon tends to be a little more expensive than other areas.

After the superb Grand'Place, the Sablon is perhaps the most distinctive old part of the city. Unlike areas whose

Antiques for sale

Place du Grand Sablon

get up and go got up and went when the focus of urban development shifted, the Sablon has gained ground and its antiques business has grown such that it has overflowed the square's boundaries in the side streets.

If you walk up from the Grand'Place, take a note for later reference of the restaurant called **La Maison Russe** at No 5 Rue de Rollebeek, whose Muscovite staff do a nice line in *blinis*. If you arrive by bus you'll get out beside the church of Notre-Dame du Grand Sablon.

There are art and antiques galleries all around the square, where you can browse freely. The weekend market seems to me more attractive, however, and the traders, whose approach is soft-sell and refined, are enthusiasts who are happy to expound on their specialty. Quality is high and not always expensive, although you're unlikely to find a Christies' piece at a *brocante* price.

Not to be missed is a visit to chocolatier and pastry-maker **Wittamer** at No 12. Belgian hand-made chocolates are generally reckoned to be the best in the world, and at Wittamer you can experience the state of the confectioner's art. Also on that side of the square are most of the chic café and restaurant terraces, where the Brussels' smart set likes to see and be seen, although these days the busy traffic passing through the square's narrow streets unfortunately makes sitting there a less pleasant experience than it should be.

Café terrace in des Jardins

Opposite Wittamer you will find the **Musée de la Poste** (Tuesday to Saturday 10am–4pm, Sunday 10am–12.30pm, closed Monday), which puts its stamp on the square with a superb collection of all things postal, from a *maquette* of the runner at Marathon to a collection of antique telephones and 1980s-vintage fax machines. A few doors along is the shopping gallery – art and antiques of course – **Les Jardins du Sablon**, with a nice under-cover *al fresco* café terrace.

Notre-Dame du Grand Sablon dominates the square with its fantastic Gothic spires and ornamentation. The church probably could do with a clean-up to fit its stylish surroundings but the stains of centuries of pollution somehow enhance its aura. It has five naves, which is said to be quite a novelty.

This brings you to the top of the Grand Sablon. Across the main road, Rue de la Régence, is the smaller **Place du Petit Sablon**. The Petit Sablon fulfils well the function of a little island of tranquillity amidst the bustle of the city. Dominated at the top end by the **Palais d'Egmont**, which is now used by the Ministry of Foreign Affairs, it has a dignified calm that endears it to the city.

On the corner of the square and Rue de la Régence is – or was, it may have moved to Place Royale by now (see *The Royal Road* in the *Day Itineraries* section) – the **Musée Instrumental** (Tuesday–Saturday 2.30pm–4.30pm, closed Monday), which houses a world-renowned collection of some 6,000 rare musical instruments, around 500 of which are usually on display.

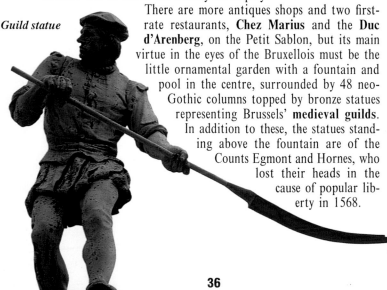

Guild statue

There are more antiques shops and two first-rate restaurants, **Chez Marius** and the **Duc d'Arenberg**, on the Petit Sablon, but its main virtue in the eyes of the Bruxellois must be the little ornamental garden with a fountain and pool in the centre, surrounded by 48 neo-Gothic columns topped by bronze statues representing Brussels' **medieval guilds**. In addition to these, the statues standing above the fountain are of the Counts Egmont and Hornes, who lost their heads in the cause of popular liberty in 1568.

2. Place Sainte-Catherine and the Lower City

In a part of the old city centre that is struggling to regain its former importance, the colourful fish-market area around Place Sainte-Catherine appears to be succeeding. Allow three hours, plus another hour or so for lunch or dinner in a seafood restaurant.

–Starting point is the Bourse–

The **Bourse**, a temple to the art of making money, is a solid-looking Second Empire-style building from 1873, fronted by Corinthian

The Bourse

columns, perhaps as a charm against the ups and downs, swings and roundabouts, to which any stock exchange is prone.

A short turn around the Bourse introduces you to some fine cafés – **Le Cirio**, **Le Grand Café** and **Falstaff** – which you will meet again at a more appropriate time (see *Café Crawl* in the *Pick & Mix* section). In case you need spiritual sustenance, there's also the atmospheric **Eglise Saint-Nicolas** on the corner of Rue au Beurre, dating from the 14th century but renovated and reconstructed several times since then. If you've a sweet tooth, there's also the old-fashioned *biscuiterie* **Dandoy** at No 31 Rue au Beurre.

Have you heard of the European capital city on the banks of the **River Senne**? No, that's not a spelling error. In days of old when knights were bold and city planners were a nightmare of the distant future, Brussels was founded on marshy ground beside the River Senne. There are old paintings in the City Museum (see *The Grand'Place* in the *Day Itineraries* section) which show a Venice-like town lapped by water.

During the 19th century, the river was channelled up, boxed off, bricked over, and generally tucked away out of sight. However, not only could it now do no harm, such as getting in the way of the *grands boulevards*, but it could also do no good by providing the kind of flowing animation that other riverside cities take for granted.

So, from the steps of the

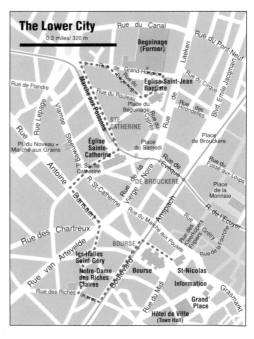

The Lower City

Bourse, cross over the river... or at least the place where it used to run, now occupied by Boulevard Anspach, taking the direction to your left for a few blocks until you reach Rue des Riches Claires where you turn right. Opposite the first crossroads are the 17th-century baroque church and convent of **Notre-Dame des Riches Claires** – or rather were until a disastrous fire burnt them to a crisp a few years back. Rebuilding has proceeded apace, however, and something approaching the original transcendence of the church and convent is being recreated.

Taking a right on Rue de la Grande-Ile, which follows the shore of one of the long-lost islands in the Senne, you arrive at **Place Saint-Géry** and the scene of a brave but doomed effort to reanimate this somewhat down-at-heel quarter. The red-brick building in the middle of the square, the Flemish neo-Renaissance-style **Marché Saint-Géry**, dating from 1881, was once a meat market. An attempt to re-establish it as **Les Halles Saint-Géry**, a Covent Garden-like centre for bijoux boutiques and cafés, sadly failed to take off despite superb restoration work. It remains to be seen what becomes of the Marché.

Facing it is the fine tavern **Le Lion d'Or** and the entrance to a cobbled courtyard where bricked-up arches indicate what became of the Senne. Next, come onto Rue Dansaert, with its more worldly (presumably successful) boutiques, until you reach the tree-lined square **Vieux Marché aux Grains**. You might want to pick up a couple of cheeses at the specialist **Crémerie de Linkebeek**, or have a snack next door at the very Brussels tavern **Le Paon Royal**.

On second thoughts, maybe you should save your appetite for one of Brussels' best restaurants, **La Sirène d'Or** at No 1A Place Sainte-Catherine. Its owner, Robert Van Duüren, was once chef to the then Prince of Liège, now King Albert II, and his seafood specialities are, well, princely. It's no coincidence that seafood is on the menu, because just around the corner is the **Marché aux Poissons**, the fish market. Actually this is less of a market than a series of shops, but what the heck, the fish are fresh and the adjoining restaurants make good use of them.

Dandoy, biscuit specialist

Before setting out down the cobbled-over street where fishing boats once docked, you might want to step into the 19th-century **Eglise Sainte-Catherine**, designed by Joseph Poelaert of

Seafood restaurants in the Lower City

Palais de Justice fame (see *The Royal Road* in the *Day Itineraries* section). The church is as grand as could be, except that the interior is spoiled by cheap plastic seats, a red carpet and a ridiculous light-sign message running across the arms of the cross.

Across from the church entrance is the remnant of an earlier baroque church, while a little further along is the **Tour Noire**, a 12th-century vestige of the original city wall, which, in a controversial decision, is being incorporated within a hotel.

Spiritually refreshed, return to the fish market with its two rectangular pools, one of which has an impressive monumental fountain mimicking the harbour that once was here. Along the streets – Quai aux Briques and Quai au Bois à Brûler – on the sides of the long cobbled rectangle are some pretty fine seafood restaurants, at least one of which offers 'takeaway lobster'. Each has a covered terrace on the cobbles. This is a good place for lunch, but it may be more atmospheric in the evening when the restaurants and terraces are all lit up. Excepting of La Sirène d'Or, which is in a class of its own, you can just about assume that the standard is similar in the others – pretty good.

Saint-Jean Baptiste

At the fountain end of the market, at **Square des Blindés**, dedicated to Belgium's armoured forces (although it has a monument to the heroic carrier pigeons of World War I), turn right onto Rue du Grand-Hospice, then Rue du Béguinage. The 17th-century baroque church of **Saint-Jean Baptiste** dominates the square ahead. From here it's just a few steps to the *béguinage*, once a medical centre for the poor, now housing the **Institut Pacheco** and a hospice for elderly people. Walk around the tranquil grounds.

39

3. The Marolles

This is a short itinerary through Brussels' old working-class Marolles district. It includes a fascinating street market that finishes at 2pm, so allow 2-3 hours in the morning depending on how much you like browsing.

–To starting point: bus 48 from the Bourse takes 15 minutes–

The Marolles is a poor part of the city in terms of income, but rich in community spirit. Marolliens are looked on as a breed apart – like London's Cockneys – with their own dialect and irreverent outlook on life. Perhaps that's why the colossal **Palais de Justice** (see *The Royal Road* in the *Day Itineraries* section) was built on a hill dominating the Marolles – to remind the lower orders who's boss. In fact, construction of the Palais took a big bite out of the original district, and the word 'architect' has been a formidable Marollien insult ever since.

It's a small district, being pressured by neighbouring affluent districts like the Sablon, which look on the Marolles' houses, shops and bars as fertile territory for expansion. Marolliens are resisting as best they can, but when 'wealth' and 'community' are weighed in the scales the long-term future must be in doubt.

The Marolles is a place for wandering in, particularly at the weekend, but there are a few landmarks which suggest a possible route. Leave the bus at the **Eglise de la Chapelle**, and walk up-hill to Place Vandervelde then turn right onto **Rue de la Samaritaine**. The houses here are typical of the Marolles, a mixture of cottages and apartments, with new developments interspersed.

In the café **Chez Jeannine** on the corner of **Rue des Chandeliers**, it is not uncommon to see suitcases on the floor – families who have lost their homes often 'live' at the neighbourhood cafés. The atmosphere in such little taverns is friendly and welcoming to strangers, so don't be bashful about going in.

Turning right on Rue du Temple brings you to **Rue Haute**, the district's main shopping street. Here, and on the parallel **Rue Blaes**, you can buy goods that cost appreciably less than the same thing in the main shopping districts. At No 132 Rue Haute is a reminder of the age and history of the Marolles, for this was once the home of the 16th-century painter Pieter Brueghel the Elder. Now the **Musée Brueghel** (1 May to 31 October weekend only 2pm–6pm for groups only, on written request), the brick-built, gabled townhouse stands out from its surroundings.

A little further along, at No 158, is Brussels' last shop selling only hats, **Miggerode**. Inside the atmospheric old shop are wooden drawers and cabinets

Flea-market figures

Old relics in the Vieux Marché

filled with Borselinos, Panamas, Brummels, Manuviers. On a bench is a little steam boiler used for shaping hats.

Just next door are **Rue de l'Epée** and **Square Pieter Brueghel**, under renovation and with a number of restaurants and café terraces, perhaps for the well-heeled denizens of the Palais de Justice which can be seen looming on its hill. The restaurants, including **Chez Lagaffe** at No 8 and the Peruvian **El Pachacamac** at No 6, and some that are typically Bruxellois, are good and not so expensive.

At the far end of Rue Haute, past the busy **Hôpital Saint-Pierre**, is a group of very reasonably priced restaurants that conjure up Spain in the heyday of cheap, mass market tourism. With names like **Alicante**, **Torremolinos**, **La Villa Rosa**, **El Rincon**, and the Portuguese **Mar Bravo**, they are a taste of the sun, and not bad either. The end of Rue Haute is the **Porte de Hal**, a massive stone gateway of the now-vanished Brussels wall. It now houses Brussels' sparsely equipped **Musée du Folklore** (Tuesday to Sunday 10am–5pm, closed Monday).

Coming back along Rue Blaes brings you quickly to **Place du Jeu de Balle**, home of Brussels' famous **Vieux Marché**, the flea-market. It seems as if nothing is too unusual for this market, much of whose goods come from the homes of the 'recently deceased'. Not perhaps the five-pointed gold-star with red ribbon of 'Hero of the Soviet Union' that I was offered, but certainly the dinner-sets, chairs, old books, paintings (well, pictures), clothes, shoes, radios, record-players, records (those quaint old vinyl things), dolls, soft toys, racing-cars (battery-operated) and everything imaginable that comes under the headings of *bric-à-brac*, junk, antiques, bargain-buys and rip-offs. In short, from 7am–2pm, all human life is there, much of it for sale, on the Place du Jeu de Balle. And even when the market has packed up there's a kind of post-market market, with the really dodgy and unsaleable stuff left lying around.

The Butte du Lion on the Waterloo battlefield

Afternoon Itineraries

4. Waterloo

Allow 3-4 hours, morning or afternoon, depending on how much walking you're prepared to do. This is where Napoleon met his Waterloo, and Wellington gave him the boot.

–To starting point: bus W from Avenue de Stalingrad beside Place Rouppe; journey takes about 40 minutes–

The Battle of Waterloo did not actually take place at Waterloo, but in rolling farmland a few kilometres to the south. So don't get off the bus in Waterloo, a busy suburb of Brussels, expecting to find the battlefield. Ask the driver to let you off instead at the **Butte du Lion**, a huge conical mound with the sculpture of a lion on top, at what was the centre of the Allied army's position.

Napoleon's troops never made it to this point on that June day in 1815; if they had there would no doubt be an eagle on the monument in place of the lion. They gave it their best shot though, and the Duke of Wellington, leading a combined force of British, Dutch and Belgians, called the bloody slaughter 'the nearest run thing you did ever see'. The timely arrival of a Prussian army clinched the matter, turning near-victory for the French into rout.

Before exploring the battlefield, study the tactical picture at the **Visitor's Centre** (1 April to 30 September 9.30am–6.30pm; 1 to 31 October 9.30am–5.30pm; 1 November to 28 February 10.30am–4pm; 1 to 31 March 10.30am–5pm) beside the bus-stop. You'll get an idea of the battle's impressive scale and emerge an instant armchair strategist, able to say where Napoleon went wrong and how you could have done better. It's cheaper to buy a combination ticket if you plan to visit more than one attraction.

Panorama of the Battle

Climbing the 226 steps of the Butte du Lion will probably leave you feeling like one of the French infantrymen who sweated up the surrounding slopes, except that you're unlikely to walk straight into a blast of musketry. The view from the summit is worth the effort, however, even if you do

need an active imagination to fill the peaceful-looking farmland with slashing cavalry charges, thundering artillery and 200,000 struggling soldiers.

Next door to the Visitor's Centre is a round-walled building containing a painted **Panorama of the Battle** (1 April to 30 September 9.30am–6.30pm; 1 to 31 October 9.30am–5.30pm; 1 November to 28 February 10.30am–4pm; 1 to 31 March 10.30am–5pm), while just across the road is a **Waxwork Museum** (1 April to 31 October 9am–6.30pm; 1 November to 31 March 10am–4.45pm, weekends 10am–4.45pm only). The circular panorama painting is spectacular, with added realism given by *maquettes* of troops, horses and equipment ranged around the viewing gallery; the Waxwork Museum is not essential unless you're fascinated by all things Napoleonic.

Take the little path beside the Panorama called the **Chemin des Vertes Bornes** and follow it past the Butte du Lion to several of Waterloo's most dramatic scenes. Beside the memorial to Lt Augustin Demulder, a young cavalryman from nearby Nivelles, massed waves of French horsemen under Marshal Ney — the 'bravest of the brave' — broke against unyielding Allied infantry squares.

A little further on, another memorial records the position of a British artillery battery that poured grape-shot into Napoleon's Old Guard, who were thrown into battle by the emperor in a desperate final effort. In contrast, the fields of corn and grass growing here today could scarcely be more tranquil. Fifteen minutes more brings you to the manor-farm of **Hougoumont**, which still bears the scars of heroic assault and valiant defence, and whose owners will let you wander around the grounds – although not into their home.

Returning to the cluster of buildings beside the Visitor's Centre, you may feel like a snack. There's no shortage of cafés and restaurants, with names like **Le Hussard**, **Bivouac de l'Empereur**, **Les Alliés**, etc. None are what you would call top-class but in typ-

Re-enacting the battle

ical Belgian style it's hard to do badly even in humble eateries, and none of them are expensive either. Souvenir shops sell everything from Napoleonic corkscrews to exquisitely hand-painted model soldiers.

Walking along the **Route du Lion** in front of the Visitor's Centre, parallel to the Allied frontline, can be about as dangerous today as it was in 1815, thanks to Belgian drivers' take-no-prisoners style. This warning applies even more if you start hopping back and forth across the **Chaussée de Charleroi** at the end of the Route. Beside this crossroads are monuments to the Belgians and Hanoverians; to Colonel Gordon, a mortally wounded aide to Wellington; and to General Picton, shot down at the head of his troops.

A little way down the hill is **La Haie-Sainte**, another of the fortified farms that played a crucial role in Napoleon's defeat, even though he eventually captured this one. In the field across the road, British cavalry slaughtered an attacking French infantry column, then got carried away with victory and charged on to the enemy artillery, which promptly blew them to pieces.

I don't recommend it, but if your blood is up you can make an hour-long trek down the Chaussée de Charleroi to **La Belle Alliance**, where Wellington and the Prussian Marshal Blücher shook hands on their victory; and to the **Wounded Eagle** monument marking the place where the Imperial Guard fought to the bitter end so that Napoleon might escape. Even more distant is **Napoleon's Headquarters**, now a museum. But without a car – or a horse – such far-flung places are none too accessible.

5. Euro-Brussels

Allow about 2 hours in the afternoon and another 2 if you include the Parc du Cinquantenaire. 'Give me liberty or give me lunch!', might easily be the rallying cry of the Eurocrats, and here you can see why.

–To starting point: metro 1A or 1B from De Brouckère station; journey takes 10 minutes–

The metro takes you to **Schuman** station, from where you emerge blinking into the light to be confronted with a spectacularly ugly grey building, like a spaceship from a planet where architects are the lowest form of

Berlaymont Palace

life set down in the middle of Brussels. This is the **Berlaymont Palace**, home of the European Commission, where all the tourists used to go to have their picture taken – until it was found to be laced with asbestos and the civil servants were evacuated.

Across the road is the ostentatious new European Union Council of Ministers building. More interesting for the visitor are the places where the civil servants take their ease. What some might call a tower of Babel, and others a colourful mixture of languages and cultures, has spawned a neighbourhood of cafés and restaurants for which cosmopolitan is an inadequate description.

Walking downhill from the Berlaymont and turning right onto **Boulevard Charlemagne**, you will find a little pub called **The Old Hack**, where English-speaking journalists (a contradiction in terms?) gather after a hard day wrestling with farm support prices and directives on how to define a pair of socks for trade purposes.

Across the road is the **International Press Centre**, where you can steal press releases on subjects such as those mentioned above.

But then, back on the other side of Boulevard Charlemagne, is a true gem, a pub called **Kitty O'Shea's** (it's Irish) which serves as fine a pint of 'mud' (Guinness) as you could hope for. You still have to listen to a certain amount of Eurobabble, but at least it's in a soft Irish lilt. Kitty's also does a good lunch and dinner.

One of the most surprising signs of the European spirit

Square Ambiorix

can be found at No 44 Boulevard Charlemagne, in **Eurotempo**, a shop devoted to selling all sorts of stuff marked with the European symbol – a circle of 12 gold stars on a blue background. Umbrellas seem especially popular. By this time you may be needing to rest your feet and the perfect place is right at hand, on **Square Ambiorix**, a miniature park that many of the civil servants use as a lunch-box. It is an elegant and pretty little place, as is its satellite a bit further downhill on **Square Marie-Louise**, which has a large pool with a fountain and grottoes. Both squares are surrounded by a dazzling array of *art nouveau* buildings. Particularly impressive is the flamboyant turn-of-the-century house of the painter **Georges de Saint-Cyr** at No 11 Square Ambiorix, designed by Gustave Strauven, a pupil of Victor Horta who was Brussels' most prolific *art nouveau* architect. Connecting the two squares is Avenue Palmerston, with a work by Horta, the **Hôtel Van Eetvelde**, now owned by a gas industry federation, which can be visited only when accompanied by an official Brussels tourist guide.

Having circled the squares, you come onto Rue Archimède, which leads to Rue Benjamin Franklin. From here return to the **Cinquantenaire**, a colossal triumphal arch surrounded by a park, which dates from 1880 when it was built to celebrate 50 years of Belgian independence.

The park entrance is a little way uphill from the Rond-Point Schuman and has the **Grande Mosquée de Bruxelles** just inside to the left. Visits can be made to the mosque, which is also an Islamic cultural centre, by appointment (tel: 735 2173).

In addition to its neo-classical, quadriga-crowned, mosaic-faced Corinthian column-flanked arch, the Cinquantenaire also houses the **Musées Royaux d'Art et d'Histoire** (open Tuesday–Friday 9.30am–5pm, weekends 10am–5pm, closed Monday), which contain a fine collection of ancient sculpture.

On the other arm of the arch is the **Musée Royal de l'Armée** (open Tuesday–Sunday 9am–noon, 1–4.45pm, closed Monday). On the other side of the courtyard is **Autoworld** (April–September 10am–6pm; October–March 10am–5pm), which is worth an afternoon jaunt, taking you through the highways and byways of automotive history.

Art nouveau at Square Ambiorix

Genval's Château du Lac

6. Lac du Genval

Allow 3 hours in the afternoon. Walking round the lake is a favourite short weekend outing for the Bruxellois.

—To starting point: Train from Gare du Nord, Gare Centrale and Gare du Midi, direction Louvain-la-Neuve; the journey takes about 40 minutes—

Genval, which means the Valley of Geneviève, is the scene of a charming legend: a young wife and her son were abandoned to their fate in the wild Fôret de Soignes by her husband, the Duke of Brabant, after she had been falsely accused of infidelity. A doe led them to a spring in a little valley, where they survived until the false accuser was found out and hanged. Geneviève was reunited with her duke – although some intensive counselling may have been needed to get their relationship back on track.

A ramp on the platform at Genval station brings you uphill, past a pharmacy, to Rue de Rosières. Turn left, following the E411 highway sign. After a ten-minute walk you will see another sign, for **Lac de Genval**, and also the lake on your left. Bear right at the lakeside. The national language divide runs across the middle of the lake, so you have to speak Dutch on the northern shore and French on the southern – *joke*.

Genval Lake is not big. You can walk around it on **Avenue du Lac** in about 40 minutes at an easy pace, but the location is idyllic and you may feel envious of the people who own all those imposing houses and villas overlooking the water. When the lake, fed by the Argentine stream, was created in 1904, the original villas replicated famous buildings. For example, the pavilion Rendez-vous d'Amour is based on an original at Versailles, while the chalet Le Rütli and the villa Guillaume Tell are based on Swiss buildings

Resting place by the lake

which are associated with William Tell (you will pass all three on this route).

Swimming in the lake is not permitted, although there is boating and fishing, and a high fountain, the **Genvaloise**, that gives the lake the aspect of a miniature Lake Geneva.

If you continue past **Le Blanc Mesnil** restaurant, the marina and some waterfront houses (including the villa Guillaume Tell) you will eventually reach a cluster of restaurants, including **Le Caraquin du Lac** for Belgian cuisine, and next door **Le Shangri-La du Lac**, an excellent Chinese restaurant with a white-painted tower, the Rendez-vous d'Amour and a waterfront terrace.

Just beyond this terrace, turn right off Avenue du Lac and follow the signs a short distance to the **Musée de l'Eau et de la Fontaine**, the water and fountain museum, (weekends and public holidays 10am–7pm). This is a curious little place, with an interesting collection of fountains as well as old water-pipes, pumps, filters and other hydraulic equipment.

Back at the lake, the shore-line is suddenly dominated by the **Château du Lac**, formerly a Schweppes bottling plant based on the design of an abbey, and now transformed into a 4-star hotel. There is an excellent restaurant, **le Trèfle à 4**, an amply stocked bar, the **Kingfisher Inn**, and mineral water from four nearby springs. The château's function suites are often booked by wedding parties. Lawn bowling and croquet are also practised at the château by the local Country Club.

Continue past the château, uphill on Avenue des Merisiers, where some of the lakeside's oldest villas are located, including the **Manoir du Lac**, an English-style country hotel. One villa, on the corner of Avenue des Sorbiers, looks like a set from a horror movie. From there it's back to towards the lake until you arrive at the point where you started.

The water and fountain museum

Savouring the fresh air

7. Green Brussels

Allow 3 hours, morning or afternoon. There are three breaths of fresh air on this route, more-or-less linked: the Etangs d'Ixelles, the Abbaye de la Cambre and the Bois de la Cambre.

—To starting point: bus 71 from Rue de l'Evêque, across Boulevard Anspach from Place de la Monnaie; journey takes about 15 minutes, depending on traffic—

The bus takes you to **Place Flagey** where the itinerary begins. Either ask the driver to tell you when you've arrived, or watch out for a square with a high brick church straight ahead of you, and trees and ponds on your right.

Those trees and ponds are where you go first, although if it's lunch-time and you're feeling peckish, you could do a lot worse than make a detour to **Le Bonaparte**, a moderately priced, typically Bruxellois café-come-restaurant at the beginning of Avenue Général de Gaulle. It's more likely, however, that you'll do the walk first, which should give you an appetite which will need to be satisfied later.

Les Etangs (ponds) **d'Ixelles** lie in a line. You can choose either bank, but as the one to your left has busy traffic and a tram line it's more restful to take Avenue Général de Gaulle which begins with a monument to the spirit of Flanders.

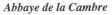
Abbaye de la Cambre

A nice aspect of Brussels is the number and quality of its green spaces – few cities of a million people can boast such a display. From the air it looks like a garden city and at places like the Ponds of Ixelles you see why. Elegant apartment blocks and town-houses on the opposite side are almost invisible behind a canopy of leaves from many different kinds of trees, yet this is in one of Brussels' busiest districts.

The ducks and swans always look pretty well-fed to me; don't feel guilty if you've nothing to give them. A little further along, another green area opens up on your right, the **Jardin du Roi** (King's Garden), given by king of the Belgians Léopold II to his no-doubt grateful subjects for their rest and enjoyment. So, rest and enjoy.

Back at the ponds again, you carry on until Rue du Levant, perhaps making a short side-step to the monument to Ixelles' colonial pioneers in the Congo (present-day Zaïre), crowned with a sculpted African's head. A more valued exponent of internationalism is remembered in adjacent Square de la Croix Rouge, with a sculpture of the Swiss founder of the Red Cross, Henri Dunant.

From the square, the arched entrance of the **Abbaye de la Cambre** is directly ahead. Many buildings of this old Cistercian abbey are in a sadly dilapidated state, although restoration is underway. But the mouldering feeling only adds to the atmosphere. A lily-covered pond, cool arbours, deep glades, an ornamental garden and the fine 13th-century church of **Nôtre-Dame de la Cambre** are packed into the grounds. Well worth seeing are the magnificent stained-glass windows behind the church altar and the smaller ones in the cloister recording the names of abbesses from 1201 to 1794.

Outside again, climb the stairs to the ornamental garden and leave by the gate just beyond the little fountain, turning right. The pavement brings you to Avenue Louise, one of Brussels' most chic streets. Directly ahead you will see **La Porte des Indes**, perhaps the best Indian restaurant this side of Bombay. At this stage in the day it's probably best just to note the location for possible future use.

Cross at the lights to the far side of Avenue Louise then turn left. A 5-minute walk brings you to the **Bois de la Cambre**, which is signposted. This park, Brussels' biggest, is the city's lung, the place where people go in good weather to sunbathe and play on the grass. Bridle-paths criss-cross it and at certain places the main roads slice through.

Following almost any path will bring you to the **Théâtre de Poche** with its nearby café terraces and roller-skating area. carrying on, you will eventually come to a small lake. A tiny electrically operated ferry makes the 2-minute voyage to **Robinson's Island**, which had a charming café/restaurant called the **Châlet Robinson** until fire transformed it into a smoking ruin. Hopefully, it is going to be rebuilt, however, and in the meantime an 'emergency service' provides refreshments from a tent. You can hire rowing and pedal boats from the island if you feel so inclined.

Parks are for wandering in, and when you've wandered until your heart's content, leave by one of the roads on the eastern side—Avenue de l'Orée or Avenue du Brésil. Then cross Avenue Franklin Roosevelt to the next parallel street where you can catch a 93 or 94 tram back to the city centre.

The Bois de la Cambre, Brussels' biggest park

Allow at least 3 hours in the afternoon for hanging on the strap of an old-time tram and a glimpse of Belgium's colonial past. If you don't go to the tram museum the trip will take an hour less.

—To starting point: metro 1B (direction Stockel) from De Brouckère station near Place de la Monnaie; journey takes about 20 minutes—

Make sure you take the correct metro because the line splits and if you mistakenly get on the 1A (as I did) you'll go in the wrong direction. Get out at **Montgomery** station and change there to the 39 or 44 tram. (If you're going direct to the Africa museum, take only the 44.) About five minutes out from Montgomery station on Avenue de Tervuren, watch for the moment when the line of apartment blocks to your left ends. Get out at the next stop and the tram museum is just behind you on the left.

The Musée du Transport Urbain

The vintage horse-drawn and electric trams at the **Musée du Transport Urbain** (first Saturday in April–first Sunday in October, weekend and public holidays only, 1.30–7pm) are a bonus on this trip, partly because of their intrinsic interest and partly because when the museum is open some of the old trams are put in service between there and the Africa museum.

If you're going direct to the Africa museum (on the 44 only), stay on until the end of the line. Although the main entrance is a little further along Tervurenlaan (street names here are in Dutch), it's better to cross over from the tram halt at the pedestrian crossing, through the side gate, towards the pavilion directly ahead, then turn left along the path past the ornamental lake and you'll see the museum entrance at the rear of the impressive neo-classical building that dominates the scene.

Life-size wildlife in the museum…

The **Musée Royal de l'Afrique Centrale** (Tuesday to Sunday, 16 March to 15 October 9am–5.30pm; 16 October to 15 March 10am–4.30pm, closed Monday) is Belgium's monument to its colonial glories in the Congo (now Zaïre), and the Belgian pioneers who 'opened up' the Dark Continent. Also included are mementoes of Henry Morton Stanley, of 'Dr Livingstone, I presume…' fame. In these enlightened times the museum has moved beyond simple imperialistic images, but rifles and artillery pieces are still displayed.

In a setting worthy of a royal country retreat, which it once was, the building is a stunning piece of architecture in the grandiose style that went down well in 1910, with a superb, naturally lit rotunda as an entrance foyer. Since Zaïre's independence in 1960, the exhibitions have broadened to include much of the rest of Africa and aspects of ethnography on a global scale. The exhibition halls feature modern African sculpture, as well as crafts, archaeology, wildlife, and environmental and development issues such as the problem of desertification.

Back outside, you can wander around the gardens and ornamental pools like landed gentry. Following the main pool across Keizerinnedreef and Spaans Huisdreef takes you to a cool forest walk, then, on the left, to a lake called the **Vijfer Van Vossem**.

A few minutes walk in the other direction along Keizerinnedreef brings you to a little waterside café called **Aan de Bootjes**. In good weather it's nice to sit on the terrace and nurse a cherry-based beer or a glass of wine before retracing your steps to the tram.

… and outside

Evening Itineraries

The 'stomach of Brussels' is another description for this restaurant-packed area of the city, but 'Ilot Sacré' sounds a lot more romantic. **Allow two hours, plus time for dining.**

–Starting point is the Place de la Monnaie–

The concentration of restaurants in the old **Ilot Sacré** – the 'Sacred Isle' – adds up to a sight worth seeing and tasting. After dark, when the restaurants are all lit up, its narrow cobbled alleys fairly glow with *bonhomie*. Some people sniffily dismiss the Ilot Sacré as a tourist-trap, but many Bruxellois like it every bit as much as the visitors, and some of the better restaurants in Brussels are here – though the very best are elsewhere.

Restaurants in the Ilot Sacré

What you get here on the Ilot Sacré, I think, is a memorable Brussels experience – generally along with some good food. Having lingered over many an *al fresco* dinner on a long summer evening in the Ilot Sacré, quietly watching the world go by and being watched in turn, I have no hesitation in pronouncing the Burgundian, Brueghelian quarter a 'must'. However, there are a few important qualifications, as we will see presently.

From **Place de la Monnaie**, take Rue des Fripiers for one block, turning left into Rue Grétry while noting the interestingly named café Drug Opera on the corner opposite. In a few steps, you walk into a kind of Bruxellois 'little Italy', where the green-white-and-red Italian colours emblazon restaurant facades and table-tops. None of them quite matches the cuisine that *mamma* used to make, and there are no *mafiosi* dining in rapture with giant napkins tucked into their shirt-fronts, but some are OK.

This first glimpse of internationalism develops as you push further into the Ilot Sacré (sometimes literally 'push', when crowds squeezing between the tables, trestles of seafood-on-ice, and platoons of waiters make passage difficult). In this culinary United Nations, there are Italian, Greek, Indian, French, Japanese, Chinese, Vietnamese, Spanish, Portuguese, Lebanese, Israeli, Moroccan, Tunisian, Caribbean, Latin American, and even some Belgian restaurants.

Crossing to **Rue des Bouchers**, you arrive at a side-alley, Impasse de la Fidelité, with a take-off of Manneken-Pis, the famous fountain in the form of a piddling little boy (see *The Grand'Place* in the *Day Itineraries* section). '**Jeanneke-Pis**' is a little girl, ditto.

Back on Rue des Bouchers is another much-loved Brussels institution, the restaurant **Chez Léon**, which specialises in seafood, especially *moules*. Chez Léon has been flexing its mussels in Brussels since 1893 and shows no signs of tiring.

The restaurant quarter continues straight ahead on Rue des Bouchers, to the left on **Rue des Dominicains** and to the right on **Petite Rue des Bouchers**. Some other typically Belgian restaurants — reasonably priced, convivial and good quality — that are well worth visiting are **Scheltema** and the *azulejos*-tiled **Rôtisserie Vincent** on Rue des Dominicains (although the latter could be a little more reasonably priced); **Aux Armes de Bruxelles** on Petite Rue des Bouchers; **Le Marmiton** near the top of Rue des Bouchers; and **De l'Ogenblik** in the **Galerie des Princes**, beside Rue des Dominicains.

In some other places — but by no means all — you may be unlucky enough to encounter high cost, brusque service and indifferent quality. Always check the menu, and 'sniff the atmosphere' before ordering; be wary if inexpensive items are, sadly, 'not available today'; check if service and value-added tax are included; always be *exactly* sure of the price of anything you order.

Part of the fun of the Ilot Sacré is to wander around and watch other people eating, while soaking up the atmosphere and honing your appetite for what's to come. Then join the crowd and tuck in. *Bon appétit!*

Part of the fun is just wandering around

10. Café Crawl

Designed to be done in the evening, this trail around some of Brussels' best city-centre cafés may leave you legless, though not because of the distance covered. Includes hints about the best Belgian beers.

–Starting point is the Gare Centrale; finishing point–that's up to you. I'm not seriously suggesting you 'do' all the cafés mentioned, or at least I don't want to be held responsible for the outcome–

It seems to me no small miracle that I am able to write about this itinery... itanariry... itinarery...

One of Brussels' special beers

tour, made on a hot summer's evening, having chosen to ignore my own sound advice about drinking only coffee, preferring instead to sample a different one of Belgium's multitudinous beers in each hostelry along the way, which has left my memory somewhat blurry, though suffused with a warm glow of appreciation.

Elsewhere, I have pointed to Belgians' love-affair with food. Like a man with two mistresses, they are equally tempted by beer. With more than 400 different varieties to choose from, most of which have their own absolutely particular and mandatory glass, including champagne glasses, it's like being a kid in Santa's toy factory. We're not talking about swilling, but about savouring carefully crafted artisanal products.

Let's begin at the beginning, with sudden death, **A la Mort Subite** at No 7 on the tastefully named Rue Montagne aux Herbes Potagères. This old tavern, a favourite among Bruxellois, is Brussels writ large. Its specialities are the traditional Brussels beers, Gueuze, Faro and Kriek, backed up by, among others, those strapping Trappist brews Chimay, Maredsous, Grimbergen and Rochefort.

The staff somehow manages to combine brusqueness with personal rapport in a way that is as disconcerting as memorable. The Mort Subite's mirrored walls, stained-glass motifs, old photographs, paintings and prints,

Cheers at the puppet-theatre Toone

plain wooden chairs and tables, and daily parade of Brussels characters, from bank managers and their mistresses to opera and ballet stars, make the perfect backdrop for a leisurely liquid break.

From here it's downhill all the way, geographically speaking, into the Galeries Saint-Hubert, then to Rue des Bouchers and Petite Rue des Bouchers, where a narrow side-alley, or Impasse, leads to **Café-Théâtre Toone**, another old, brown, wood-panelled institution, this time with a sophisticated puppet theatre attached.

Having earlier witnessed sudden death, we might as well move on to the coffin – across Rue du Marché aux Herbes into Rue des Harengs, to No 10. The atmosphere at **Le Cerceuil** (The Coffin) is a bit dead, but that's the idea. You walk down a purple-painted hallway, serenaded by funereal music, and sit at a coffin-lid table to which the waiter brings your beer in a skull-shaped pitcher (although only if you ask, and pay extra, for one). Le Cerceuil is worth a visit, if only to say you've had a skullful rather than a skinful.

From there it's but a short step to the Grand'Place, whose cafés are the most obvious ones to visit – **Le Roy d'Espagne**, **La Brouette** and **La Chaloupe d'Or**. Nev-

ertheless, particularly in fine weather, when the café terraces spread out over the cobblestones, this makes for one of the most memorable places to nurse a Belgian beer while watching the world – or at least a fair part of it – pass by.

Retrace your (probably by this time rather uncertain) steps to Rue du Marché aux Herbes, and the alley-end café **Au Bon Vieux Temps** at No 12. If brown is your

Falstaff opened in 1904

favourite café colour and traditional your favourite style, you'll be in hog-heaven here. Should the good old days ever return, they'll probably begin in such a place, and probably be discovered drinking a glass of Duvel beer.

Toddle down to Rue de la Bourse and its two outstanding cafés, Le Cirio and Le Grand Café. I prefer Le Cirio, whose respectable clientele seem to offer an admirable role model. Le Grand Café is at least *fairly* grand, with its balustraded second floor.

Finally, on the other side of the Bourse, we arrive at the star of the show: the **Falstaff**. A fancifully eclectic mix of *art deco*, *art nouveau* and rococo style – Falstaff opened its doors in 1904 and has been serving up turn-of-the-century ambiance ever since. Its waiters are widely considered to be the stuffiest, most maddeningly self-absorbed and arrogant in the country – which is no mean commendation. Personally, I've always found them eager to please, just as farmers are with their turkeys a few days before Christmas. But please don't tell them I said so.

1. Bruges

This is one of Europe's most perfectly preserved medieval cities, whose canals only add to the visual delight. The day-long trip includes the option to visit nearby Damme, an equally charming Flemish village.

—To starting point: Train from Gare du Nord, Centrale or Midi; journey takes about 1 hour—

Bruges is a Flemish town whose real name is **Brugge**. Thinking 'Brugge' will add to your understanding, as well as helping you get off at the correct railway station because the destination boards say Brugge.

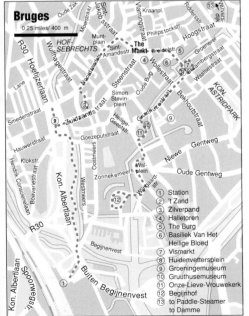

Bruges
0.25 miles/ 400 m

① Station
② 't Zand
③ Zilverpand
④ Halletoren
⑤ The Burg
⑥ Basiliek Van Het Heilige Bloed
⑦ Vismarkt
⑧ Huidenvettersplein
⑨ Groeningemuseum
⑩ Gruuthusemuseum
⑪ Onze-Lieve-Vrouwekerk
⑫ Begijnhof
⑬ to Paddle-Steamer to Damme

This is a small city which discourages cars, so it is pleasant to walk through its central district. But it is also useful to get a feel for Brugge outside the centre, where the lucky inhabitants have a historical treasure all to themselves. Brugge rewards aimless wandering as well as careful itinerary-following.

From Stationsplein, take the pathway through the park on the left of the canal and follow it to a wide square called **'t Zand**. A facing street, the **Vrijdagmarkt**, indicates that this was once where the Friday Market was held, and

The Markt

the square's size gives some idea of what an event this must have been. There's now a Saturday-morning market here. As well as graceful houses, cafés, shops and restaurants, 't Zand's most notable feature is the large modern sculpture group and fountain complex in the middle.

Zuidzandstraat, then Zilverstraat, with a diversion through the Zilverpand shopping gallery, brings you, via Noordzandstraat and Sint-Amandstraat, to the **Markt**. This beautiful square, with heraldic banners floating from its facades, is dominated–as indeed the whole city is–by the **Halletoren** (April to September 9.30am–5pm; October to March 9.30am–12.30pm, 1.30–5pm). The **Belfry**, all 79 metres (260ft) of it, has 366 interior steps leading to a 47-bell carillon served by a full-time carillonist.

Below the Belfry are the **Hallen**, formerly used by traders and for fairs. The complex dates from the 13th to the 15th century, with later additions due to fire. An equally ornate building in neo-Gothic style on the adjacent side of the square is the **Provinciaal Hof**, the government building of West Flanders Province.

Breidelstraat, at the side of the Halletoren, takes you to Brugge's most historic square, the **Burg**, from where the horse-and-carriage city tours leave. Side-by-side in this small space are superb buildings that span the centuries from the 14th to the 19th, and even include a reasonable effort from the 20th. Pride of place must go to the Romanesque **Basiliek van het Heilige Bloed** (April to September 9.30am–noon, 2–6pm; October to March 9.30am–12.30pm, 1.30–5pm), which houses a **Relic of the Holy Blood** reputedly brought to Brugge in 1149, after the Second Crusade.

'Medieval' Bruges

To the left of this atmospheric old church is the City Hall, the **Stadhuis** (April to October 9.30am–5pm; November to March 9.30am–12.30pm, 1.30–5pm), a refined-looking 14th-century building in Gothic style. Its magnificent Gothic Hall is particularly worth seeing for its wall-paintings and wood-vaulted ceiling.

In this trip down architecture's memory lane, you might also want to note the Burg's 16th-century Flemish Renaissance-style **Oude Griffie** (Old Recorders' House), the 17th-century baroque **Proosdij** (Deanery) and the 18th-century neoclassical **Gerechtshof** (Court of Justice). And if all that architecture leaves you somewhat dry, help is at hand in the brasserie **Tom Pouce** (20th-century down-the-hatch style).

Leave the Burg by Blinde-Ezelstraat and cross the bridge over the canal. On your right is the first of several landing stages for the canal-boat trips of Brugge, one of which you ought to make,

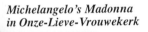

Michelangelo's Madonna in Onze-Lieve-Vrouwekerk

although I suggest you wait until after lunch when sore feet and a full stomach will probably make you ready for the break.

To your left you have the covered **Vismarkt** from 1821, where on most mornings you can treat yourself to the sight of fish being disembowelled before your very eyes and, in the case of *haring* (herring), often going straight into the bowels of the nearest human.

To the right is the magic little **Huidenvettersplein**, where the tanners used to have their guild-house, now a restaurant, and tanned the hide of any cow which happened to wander past. Now tourists on the café terraces do something similar with their own hides, while artists record the scene for posterity and a bunch of thousand-franc notes.

If you think Brugge has been picturesque up until now (and if you don't you're living on the wrong planet), you haven't seen anything yet. But you will, as soon as you emerge onto **Rozenhoedkaai**, with its view over the canal, the old waterside houses and the Belfry. Taking a break at the corner café **'t Klein Venetie** is maybe a little obvious, but the outlook makes up for the lack of adventure.

Keep along the canal to the **Dijver**, a tree-shaded bank where the weekend antiques and flea market is held. This leads to the **Groeninge-museum** (April to October 9.30am–5pm; November to March 9.30am–12.30pm, 2–5pm, closed Tuesday), the fine arts museum, which houses, among other periods, a superb collection of works by the 'Flemish primitives', including Jan van Eyck, Hans Memling and Rogier Van der Weyden.

Coming back to the Dijver, then Gruuthusestraat, take the little alleyway past the **Brangwynmuseum**, dedicated to the works of English artist Frank Brangwyn who, for some reason, was a big hit in Brugge. The courtyard leads to the **Gruuthusemuseum**, once the 15th-century palace of the Lords of Gruuthuse, who had a lu-

Night view looking towards the Belfry

crative monopoly on *gruut*, a blend of herbs and spices for improving the taste of beer (as in 'This beer tastes nice and gruuty').

Pass through the grove of lime trees and squeeze through the narrow gap between the palace and **Onze-Lieve-Vrouwekerk** (April to September 10–11.30am, 2.30–5pm, Sunday 2.30–5pm; October to March 10–11.30am, 2.30–4.30pm, Sunday 2.30–4.30pm). Inside the church, behind protective glass, is a *Madonna and Child* by Michelangelo, one of the few works by the Renaissance master that rests outside Italy. The smallish Carrara marble sculpture is spellbindingly beautiful.

Come out onto Katelijnestraat and turn right into **Stoofstraat**, whose public bath-house that allowed mixed bathing used to bask in a steamy reputation until it was closed down when the authorities decided that the proverbial proximity of cleanliness and godliness was no longer apparent.

Spirituality, however, was very much in evidence a little way off, across Walplein, onto Wijngaardstraat and over the bridge, at the **Begijnhof** (April to September 9.30am–noon, 1.45–5.30pm, Sunday 10.45am–noon, 1.45–6pm; October to March 10.30am–1noon, 1.45–5pm). Founded in the 13th century, this tranquil corner continued until recent times as a home for *begijns*, religious women similar to nuns, except that while they vowed chastity and obedience they drew the line at poverty. The Begijnhof is now a Benedictine convent.

Canal tour

It'll now be lunchtime (or possibly midnight if you've lingered on the way), time to come back, perhaps by a different route, to **Huidenvettersplein** for lunch on a café terrace. Af-

Damme paddle steamer

ter that, take a 40-minute boat tour from nearby **Landing Stage 1**. You'll cover much of the same ground, or rather water, as in the morning but from a uniquely satisfying angle.

Then just wander around, keeping your eyes open, making your own discoveries. If you want a suggestion, start from the Burg and take Hoogstraat, Verversdijk, then the long and elegant **Pottereirei**. This canalside walk will take at least half an hour and put you close to the landing-stage on Noorweegse Kaai from where a stern-wheel paddle-steamer, the *Lamme Goedzaak*, makes excursions along the canal to **Damme**, a Flemish village renowned for its good restaurants.

Time constraints may mean taking a taxi to Brugge for dinner (try the canalside terrace of **'t Bourgoensche Cruyce** at No 41 Wollestraat or **De Stove** at No 4 Kleine Sint-Amandstraat). Then it's time for the last train back to Brussels.

2. Spa

Discover the origins of mineral springs resorts at their source. Allow a whole day, and be prepared to do a fair amount of walking to get the most from the trip.

–To starting point: Train from Gare du Nord, Gare Centrale or Gare du Midi, direction Liège-Welkenraedt or Köln; journey takes about 2 hours–

The two-hour journey includes a change at **Verviers** then a 15-minute ride on a local train to **Spa**. This is a long day, so start early, but I've done it often enough myself.

The *Oxford Dictionary* defines a spa as 'a place where there is a curative mineral spring (from Spa in Belgium)', and the town virtually floats on some of the healthiest H_2O ever to bubble up to the surface. Its springs have been celebrated since Roman times. Then, from the 16th century onwards, leading figures of church and state came to take the waters, and maybe put a little iron in their souls.

Spa: Morning

0.25 miles/ 400 m

Avenue des Platanes
Parc de Sept Heures
R. Brixhe
Rue Delhasse
Pouhon Prince de Condé
Promenade des Français
Pt. Royale
Pouhon Pierre-Le-Grand
Musée de la Ville d'Eaux
Chapelle
Casino
R. Albin Body
Bains
Rue Servais
Av. Reine Astrid
Rue de la Sauvenière
Station
Pl. des Ecoles
Spa Monopole
Château d'Eau
Blvd. Chapman
Avenue des Lanciers
Av. Marie Therese
Av. Antoine
Av. de Pierre Gaspar
Route de la Géronstère
Blvd. Lühr
Rue de Barisart
Blvd. des Guérets
Boulevard Rener
Av. Potier
Chemin du Fawley
Avenue Professeur Henrijean
Ruisseau du Vieu Spa
Chemin de la Herde

- - - AM
- - - PM

↓ see map: Spa: Afternoon

Casanova, Descartes and Victor Hugo all came to Spa

One such was Tsar Peter the Great, suffering from what, in polite circles, was called 'a digestive complaint', Peter lapped up great quantities of Spa's premier cru and proclaimed his imperial flatulence at an end, so to speak. After that, any aristocrat worth his salt took his tummy troubles to Spa. So there you are, on the platform at Spa station, following, more or less, in such distinguished footsteps. What's the first thing you notice? Probably the smell. No, nothing to do with Peter the Great: rather there's a pleasantly sharp tang. Spa is set among the piney forests of Belgium's **Ardennes** region – noted for its scenic and culinary delights – and all those trees suffuse the air with scent.

Exit the station and go downhill to Avenue Reine Astrid. Cross the road to the **Musée de la Ville d'Eaux** (15 June to 15 September, plus Easter and Christmas school vacations, 2.30–5.30pm). Continue along Avenue Reine Astrid for five minutes until you arrive at **Place Royale**, where you will find the tourism office at the end of the pavilion to your left. Pick up a street map and an information brochure. The portico behind the tourism office is where you will find a Sunday-morning flea-market, and around it is the elegant **Parc de Sept Heures** where Victorian-era *curistes* used to stroll between baths.

A fashionable place to be

Just beyond Place Royale, fronting Rue Royale, is the heart of the 19th-century resort, the neoclassical **Thermal Establishment** (with the word BAINS carved on the tympanum). On weekdays, depending on how busy they are, it may be possible, for a small charge, to take a relaxing bath here in naturally carbonated mineral water from the nearby moorlands.

Beside the Thermal Establishment are the **Casino** and the **Theatre**, both looking a little the worse for wear and indicating that Spa has gone downhill since its *belle epoque* heyday.

At the end of Rue Royale you come to an airy pavilion called the **Pouhon Pierre le Grand** – *pouhon* is the local (Walloon) word for a metallic spring; Pierre, of course, was the dyspeptic Tsar Of All The Russias – Peter the Great. For a nominal charge you can drink as much of the odiferous trickle as you care to – I'm willing to bet it won't be much. You should keep the beaker you'll be given for later use.

If you still have an hour or so before lunch, you might want to backtrack to Place Royale, turn left along Rue Albin Body, then right onto Rue Auguste Laporte. Directly ahead is the bottling plant of **Spa Monopole**, the company that exploits the surrounding mineral water resources.

Tasting the waters

You can take a tour (Monday to Friday 9–11.30am, 1–3.30pm, except Christmas week) and drown in the rain of statistics poured forth by the guide: '30 springs, peak output 6 million bottles and cans per day, which is 5 million litres of water, or 250,000 cases, or 300 truckloads'.

For a light lunch, I suggest the **Chalet du Parc** in Parc de Sept Heures. It's not Spa's best restaurant, but it's in a relaxing location and will get you on your way again fairly quickly.

Now it's time for some more walking. Back to Place Royale, then Place Verte and Place de la Providence, to Rue de Barisart. This begins the **Route des Sources**, a tour of the principal springs. A 45-minute walk on this road, up through the town and into the countryside, brings you to the **Source de Barisart**, one of the commercially bottled springs. You can rest for a moment at the café there and pop down to the spring for a beaker of refreshing water.

Follow the yellow sign pointing up though the forest to the **Fontaine de la Géronstère**, your next port of call, about 30 minutes away. The path

En route to the Fontaine de la Géronstère

among the trees is just one of many promenades that have been marked out in the forests around Spa, so be sure to follow the correct yellow indicator sign. Here, the water arrives in a grotto beside a fine, reasonably priced country restaurant, **La Géronstère**.

Cross the main road outside the restaurant, following the signs for Sauvenière. A dead-straight road through the forest takes you past the **Arboretum of Tahanfagne**, noted for its variety of trees, but I suggest you consult with your leg muscles before making any diversions. It'll be another 30 minutes or so before you're at the side-by-side **Fontaine de la Sauvenière** and **Fontaine de Groesbeeck**, which are also side-by-side with another fine restaurant.

From here it's downhill all the way, on Avenue Peltzer de Clermont, to the **Fontaine du Tonnelet**. In this case, the restaurant, **La Fontaine du Tonnelet**, is Italian, excellent, and, if you have arrived in the late afternoon, closed. Console yourself with a final taste of mineral water from the adjacent red-and-white painted pavilion. The harder it is to swallow, the better it is for you.

Continue downhill, turning right onto Chemin de Prefayhai, then right again onto Avenue Marie Henriette, to the main road. To the left, it's a short walk back to Spa, but if you feel up to it, going to the right on the lower road involves a 20-minute jaunt to the **Lac de Warfaaz**, where you can take the weight off your feet at a lakeside terrace or in one of the reasonably good restaurants across the way. It may be an idea to ask about the time of the next (infrequent) bus back to Spa centre before getting too settled, although you could always call for a taxi — or even walk!

Spa: Afternoon

0.8 miles/ 1300 m

BOIS DE LA LONGUE HEID
Avenue Princesse Clémentine
Av. Gustave III
Château d'Eau
Lac de Warfaaz
HEID-FANARD
SPALOUMONT
Avenue Léopold II
Avenue Maraifagne
Avenue Hesse
Fontaine du Tonnelet
CIMETIÈRE
PRÉFAYEHAY
Spa
v. Reine Astrid
Chapelle
Av. Elisabeth
Route du Tonnelet
Château Le Haut-Neubois Home
Château d'Eau
Route de la Sauvenière
WATROOZ
Chapelle
Fontaine de la Sauvenière et de Groesbeek
Chapelle
Vieille Route de Stavelot
Route de Machamps
Route des Guérets
BOIS DE BELLE HEID
Château d'Alsa
LA HAVETTE
Av. Belle Reid
OCTAISART
Château de Meyerbeer
LE THIER DE STATTE
BARISART
Source de Barisart
Route des Fontaines
BOIS Arboretum de Tahanfagne
Chemin des Minières
Chem. des Sables
BOIS DE MAMBAYE
Route de la Géronstère
Chem. de la Géronstère
DE LA PICHEROTTE
BOIS DE LA GÉRONSTÈRE
Fontaine de la Géronstère
LA GÉRONSTÈRE

Shopping

The main shopping districts detailed below represent good itineraries all by themselves, except that there's not much more to see than shops. They sell specialty Belgian products, including lace, crystal, diamonds, chocolates, beers, and foodstuffs such as cheeses, Ardennes hams and pâté.

Non-EU residents may be able to claim back some of the tax they pay on purchases. It's worth asking about this in the main shopping areas, particularly if you're buying a lot. Given that Brussels is not so big, it has enough shopping prospects to keep the most avid buyer busy.

If you're looking for a bargain, the magic words to watch for are *soldes* and *solden*. Even better, though rarer, are *liquidation totale* and *totaal uitverkoop*, announcing that everything must go.

Rue Neuve

What this area lacks in cool sophistication – and it lacks a lot – it makes up for in popular prices. Beginning at Place Rogier, there is the **Centre Rogier** – but I can't say I care for its cheap 'n' tacky 'charm' and I don't think you will either. So let's cross the road to **City 2**, three floors of shopping-mall hustle and bustle, where anything that can be carried can be bought, along with a lot that needs to be delivered. Everything is under the one roof, with all the supporting necessities like pizzerias, hot-dog stalls, ice-cream parlours, coffee stands and bar terraces.

There are masses of shops of all varieties in City 2. Especially notable are FNAC, Belgium's good-value books-magazines-CDs-computer-video-photo shop (you can also buy concert tickets); **Weyn's** honey shop, where even sweet preparations for your feet are on sale; **Le Jardin d'Apollon**, which specialises in bonsai trees; and **Inno**, Belgium's premier department store.

If you need fresh air, come out onto **Rue Neuve**, where you can buy all the same things again, maybe even at a slightly keener

Brussels is rightly celebrated for its lace

price, and bump shoulders with people jostling their way along the narrow, pedestrian-only precinct. Or side-step to the parallel **Boulevard Adolphe Max** for more of the same.

At the far end of Rue Neuve, past another entrance to Inno, are more department stores, **C&A**, **Marks and Spencer**, **Peek & Cloppenburg** (P&C) and **Sarmalux**. And if that's not enough, you then arrive at two more multi-level shopping malls, the **Centre Monnaie** and the **Anspach Center**, to relieve you of the last few francs in your wallet or purse.

In the Centre

With the real mass shopping left behind at Rue Neuve, the pace slows a little. On Rue des Fripiers are some small clothes boutiques,

Galeries Saint-Hubert

like **Ragazzi** and **Kookaï**, and a charming little toy shop, **In Den Olifant**. **Samoka** is a place to rest over a cup of fresh-milled coffee, or linden tea.

The **Galerie du Centre** attracts a regular clientele, thanks in part to its **Leonidas** pralines shop, serving up some of the best of those dangerously wonderful Belgian chocolates. The male half of any shopping duo may like to know that one exit from the Galerie leads straight into **Au Bon Vieux Temps**, a typical Brussels bar (I suggest a Duvel beer if it's been a tough outing).

Rue de Tabora sports the excellent **Nicolas** wine shop and **Le P'tit Normand** cheeses. On Rue du Marché aux Herbes, you have **Michelangeli**, for perfumey handbags, drapes and teddy bears; and further up there's **Eurolines**, with everything you never really wanted to own, sporting the blue-and-gold Eurosymbol. **Dandoy**, on neighbouring Rue au Beurre is the place for sweet-tooth biscuit specialities like *speculoos* and *pain à grecque*.

If you hadn't taken Rue du Marché aux Herbes, you'd have come to Rue du Midi, where the quietly fanatical stamp and coin dealers are, along with the occasional surgical supports and toilet furnishings shop.

Galeries Royales Saint-Hubert

Europe's first shopping mall, built between 1846 and 1847 in an Italian neo-Renaissance style, the **Galeries** offer classy shopping – but at a price. Here are **Häagen-Dazs** for ice-cream; **Oriande** for crystal and jewellery; **Libraire des Galeries** for books on art; **Tropismes** for paperbacks; **Ganterie Italienne** for gloves; **Delvaux** for leather goods; and **Neuhaus** for chocolates.

Rue Antoine Dansaert

The modish boutiques on Rue Antoine Dansaert, across from the Bourse, seem to come and go but the designers retain some of the reputation for brashness that made such a fresh impact on the fashion scene in recent years. Stephane Kélian and Farrutx have departed, but **Gala**, **Stijl** and

Leather bags from Delvaux

Romeo Gigli remain, as well as **Kat** (for kids). At No 6 there's the almost painfully smart café **L'Archiduc**, and some trendy eateries like La Femme du Boulanger and Le Pain Quotidien.

Porte de Namur

This is the main upmarket shopping district and includes the nearby **Avenue de la Toison d'Or;** the **Boulevard de Waterloo** opposite, with even further upmarket boutiques; and parts of nearby **Avenue Louise** and **Place Stéphanie**. Belgian fashion designer **Olivier Strelli** sets out his 'stall' on Avenue Louise, while other well-known names like **Gucci**, **Gianni Versace** and **Nina Ricci** find Boulevard de Waterloo more to their taste. On their side of the road, just before the Hilton Hotel, the tranquil little Jardin d'Egmont is a good place to take a break – it's not a shop, but a park.

On the other side of the road, the facades are punctuated with gallery entrances leading to a glittering maze of shops. From Place Stéphanie there is **Galerie Louise**, **Espace Louise**, **Galerie de la Toison d'Or** (Gallery of the Golden Fleece), appropriately named, perhaps, and **Galerie Porte de Namur**.

Eating

Did someone mention eating out? *Now* you're talking. Eating out is Brussels' home turf. Home is where the heart is and wherever Brussels' heart leads, the stomach won't be far behind. Good food is more than a passion; you could say it's Brussels' pride and joy.

The difficulty is where to begin. The Sablon area perhaps, where art and antiques dealers rub shoulders with restaurateurs; seafood at Place Sainte-Catherine; the Grand'Place, Ilot Sacré (but be discriminating), or Galeries Saint-Hubert; you could venture into Ixelles and Uccle, where good restaurants are as common as lamp-posts; or walk into the first eatery you see and test my theory that it's just about impossible to eat badly in Brussels.

Eating ethnic is no great difficulty when a quarter of the population is foreign. An enclave of Indian and Pakistani restaurants is taking shape on Chaussée de Louvain, not far from a Turkish quarter on Chaussée de Haecht. Greek, Spanish, Italian, Portuguese, French, American, Asian – take your pick.

Specialities from Brussels itself and of Flanders and Wallonia are many and varied: *stoemp*, puréed vegetables to accompany steaks and stews; *witloof*, chicory or Belgian endive; herring, raw with onion; sole (*à l'Ostendaise*); *moules*, mussels, which Belgians have made their own even if they do come from Holland; cheeses, more than 300 varieties; beers, more than 400. These few words do but little justice to an entire universe of *artisanale* cuisine.

Price categories below are based on the average cost of a three-course meal for two with a bottle of wine: £ = £25–50; ££ = £50–75; £££ = £75–120; ££££ = more than £125. Taking the business lunch or fixed menu could drop the price by one category.

Restaurants
Stellar Brussels

COMME CHEZ SOI
23 Place Rouppe
Tel: 512 2921
Master chef Pierre Wynants' small and intimate holy-of-holies serves the finest French cuisine this side of heaven, in a Horta-style *salle*. Unforgettable, but reserve well in advance or forget it. ££££.

Pierre Wynants of Comme Chez Soi

EDDIE VAN MAELE
964 Chaussée Romaine
Tel: 460 6145
Just beyond the Parc des Expositions at the Heysel. Van Maele has applied the laid-back experience gained during sojourns in America to his rather-more-than-nouvelle cuisine. ££££.

LA SIRENE D'OR
1A Place Sainte-Catherine
Tel: 513 5198
There will be few siren voices following a trip to this restaurant, near the Marché aux Poissons where fishing boats once landed their catch. Now, master chef Robert Van Duüren hauls in culinary devotees with his excellent seafood. £££.

Traditional Brussels

'T KELDERKE
15 Grand'Place
Tel: 513 7344
Plain, hearty Belgian fare such as *stoemp*, *carbonnades* and *moules*, served in a convivial, low-ceilinged cellar with the kitchen in plain view, and the Grand'Place nearby for an after-dinner stroll. £.

IN 'T SPINNEKOPKE
1 Place du Jardin aux Fleurs
Tel: 511 8695
One of Brussels' oldest restaurants, which proudly proclaims its affinity with traditional Bruxellois beers. Serves Belgian specialities like *waterzooi op Gentse wijze* and *moules à la Maredsous* in a plainly furnished room with mirrored walls. £.

Au Vieux Bruxelles
35 Rue Saint-Boniface
Tel: 513 0181
Any Bruxellois *moules*-fancier worth his salt-water passion reveres this 1880s restaurant where, amidst Old Brussels decor, mussels are served in 15 different ways in an atmosphere that somehow combines hallowed silence with a buzz of friendly conversation. £.

Chez Leon
18 Rue des Bouchers
Tel: 511 1415
A Brussels institution since 1893; specialises in massive mussels for Belgian aficionados who curl their lips at the diminutive creatures favoured by the French. £.

La Roue d'Or
26 Rue des Chapeliers
Tel: 514 2554
The brasserie decor is a mixture of mirrored *art nouveau* and homage to Magritte. Service and atmosphere are familiar-and-friendly Brussels and the food is ace. ££.

Mirabelle
49 Chaussée de Boondael
Tel: 649 5173
Located relatively near the campus of

The Ilot Sacré

the Université Librede Bruxelles, this is representative of the good-value restaurants in an area frequented by students and Bruxellois-in-the-know. £.

French Style

La Quincaillerie
45 Rue du Page
Tel: 538 2553
Perhaps a little too conscious of its own modish good looks, this brasserie is in a renovated hardware store with the drawers and cupboards still in place. Nevertheless, when it comes to taste, it delivers. ££.

Scheltema
7 Rue des Dominicains
Tel: 512 2084
One of the Ilot Sacré restaurants that have not allowed the easy tourist market to demean its standards of service, quality and price. Its style and animated location complement seafood specialities. ££.

La Truite d'Argent

23 Quai aux Bois à Brûler
Tel: 218 3926

La Truite d'Argent has an attractive old interior, plus a terrace on the historic Marché aux Poissons. Youthful owner Michel Smeesters relishes the history and traditions of the place. His seafood specialities are highly recommended. ££.

L'Ogenblik

1 Galerie des Princes
Tel: 511 6151

Offers a Parisienne bistro-style ambience despite its semi-Dutch name ('Blink of an Eye'), with one foot in the elegant Galeries Saint-Hubert, one in the mainstream Ilot Sacré. Food is of a high standard, well presented and served by helpful staff. £££.

Le Marmiton

43A Rue des Bouchers
Tel: 511 7910

Trencherman quantity combines with good quality at a reasonable price. If all Ilot Sacré restaurants maintained the high standards of Le Marmiton, there would be no reason for warning visitors to the area to be on their guard against sharp operators. ££.

Ethnic

Passage To India

223 Chaussée de Louvain
Tel: 735 3147

Unpretentious Indian restaurant which has won a following for its thoughtful presentation of a great culinary tradition. £.

Le Cambodge

77 Rue Washington
Tel: 537 7098

The light, airy decor works well with the Cambodian cuisine. Terrace. £.

Le Karibu

344 Chaussée de Wavre
Tel: 230 3379

A taste of Belgium's colonial days in Zaïre. But independence is guaranteed, along with exotic delicacies like crocodile, capitaine and tilapia, washed down with Tembo beer. ££.

Rick's Cafe Americain

344 Avenue Louise
Tel: 647 7530

Ethnic? An American restaurant? In this context, yes. A little bit of Bogie swagger to go along with the burgers and Tex-Mex food. ££.

Nightlife

Brussels' venues for 'high' culture are about all that could be desired for a city of 1 million people; in the Théâtre Royal de la Monnaie Brussels has one of Europe's outstanding opera and ballet houses. Under the direction of Gérard Mortier, the opera consistently broke new ground, while the dance section was temporary 'home' to Maurice Béjart and Mark Morris. Mortier has moved to the Salzburg Festival but there seems little doubt that the Monnaie will continue to thrive.

Theatre too is vigorous enough, and if most of it is in French or Flemish that's hardly Brussels' fault. The city already makes enough concessions to English – almost every single cinema shows films in their original language, which invariably means English.

Jazz must be Brussels' other love. As well as the annual Audi and Brosella jazz festivals and the Jazz Rallye, there is a steady diet of good music throughout the year. And Brussels' fascination with cafés has gone beyond the neighbourhood local, enough to generate a stylish and animated scene, often with music attached.

For what's on information, consult the newspapers *Le Soir* and *De Standaard*, or the weekly English-language *The Bulletin*.

In the Black Bottom Cabaret

Camp caberet at a downtown transvestite club

Classical Music

PALAIS DES BEAUX-ARTS
23 Rue Ravenstein
Tel: 507 8200
The main venue for classical music and home of the Belgian National Orchestra.

CIRQUE ROYALE
81 Rue de l'Enseignement
Tel: 218 2015
Also features other kinds of music, along with theatre, dance and opera.

CONSERVATOIRE ROYAL DE MUSIQUE
30 Rue de la Régence
Tel: 511 0427
Brussel's premier venue for chamber music.

Ballet and Opera

THEATRE ROYAL DE LA MONNAIE
Place de la Monnaie
Tel: 218 1211
A superb setting for both ballet and opera, the Monnaie is the glittering star in the city's cultural firmament. The theatre also acts as a venue for classical music.

Theatre

THEATRE 140
140 Avenue Plasky
Tel: 733 9708
Performances of modern theatre and dance.

THEATRE VARIA
78 Rue du Sceptre
Tel: 640 8258
Like Théâtre 140, Varia is also good for modern theatre and dance.

THEATRE TOONE VII
21 Petite Rue des Bouchers
Tel: 511 7137
A folklore puppet theatre, attached to a fine old bar. Although not specifically for children, youngsters are sure to enjoy the shows.

Théâtre de la Monnaie

Night time in the city

THÉÂTRE ROYAL DU PARC
3 Rue de la Loi
Tel: 511 4149
An important venue for mainstream theatre, located across the road from Parliament.

KONINKLIJKE VLAAMSE SCHOUWBURG
146 Rue de Laeken
Tel: 217 6937
Fancy a taste of Flemish theatre? This is the place to go. Performances are in Dutch.

KAAITHEATER
20 Place Sainctelette
Tel: 212 5959
As with the Koninklijke Vlaamse Schouwburg (above), but inclined towards avant-garde material.

Nightclubs and Discos

MIRANO CONTINENTAL
38 Chaussée de Louvain
Tel: 218 5772
This is the smartest dance-venue in town, where the young and hip can admire each other – and themselves, of course.

CARTAGENA
70 Rue Marché au Charbon
Only hot-blooded Latin types need apply - along with all those cool north-erners whose blood could use a little extra heat.

LE GARAGE
18 Rue Dusquenoy
Tel: 512 6622
This nightclub appears to have lost its appeal to Brussels' ultra-chic crowd. Nonetheless its near-Grand'Place location ensures it remains a popular disco with tourists and is usually crowded. Sunday evenings are reserved for gays only.

L'ECUMES DES NUITS
122a Galerie Louise
Tel: 512 9147
Here the ambience is funky African and Caribbean.

SAINT-TROPEZ
16 Grand'Place
Tel: 513 7276
It may not seem a wonderful idea to have a disco in this venerable square, but they have to go somewhere and this is a good one.

FUNNY HORSE
37 Rue de Livorne
Tel: 649 8416
A traditional type of place which insists on men wearing a suit and tie. It attracts both the young and the not-so young.

Jazz

PRESERVATION HALL
3 Rue de Londres.
Tel: 511 0304.
This is a suitably smoky and crowded venue with lots of atmosphere. Its programme changes frequently but the quality is always high. It occasionally features musicians from its famous namesake in New Orleans.

NEW YORK CAFE JAZZ CLUB
5 Chaussée de Charleroi
(Place Stephanie)
Tel: 534 8509
A modern setting and perhaps a little too cool and trendy for its own good, but that is no reflection on its choice of music, which is consistently high.

Blues

BLUES CORNER
12 Rue des Chapeliers
Tel: 511 9274
Dark, dingy, smoky, noisy, crowded — just about perfect in fact for some fine blues licks.

Cabaret

BLACK BOTTOM
1 Rue du Lombard
Tel: 511 0608
Small, raffish and atmospheric, this Parisienne-style club offers piano cabaret. Compères Jerry and Martigny keep things moving in a languid sort of way.

LE SHOW POINT
14 Place Stéphanie
Tel: 511 5364
This is a glitzy, platinum-card type of place, with lots of heavily made-up girls 'go-go' dancing and others waiting in an interested sort of way outside.

Cinemas

UGC DE BROUCKERE
38 Place de Brouckère
Tel: 218 0434
Newly rebuilt 8-screen complex in the centre.

KINEPOLIS
Bruparck Centre
Tel: 478 0450
This is the biggest cinema complex in the world, they say. It has a staggering 29 screens and an IMAX 'wrap-around' theatre.

ACROPOLE
8 Avenue de la Toison d'Or
Tel: 511 432.
This complex has 11 screens. It is located in the uptown area near Avenue Louise.

Café-terrace jazz

Calendar of Special Events

As a city with a proud cultural tradition to celebrate, there is scarcely a moment when some special event is not taking place in Brussels. Folkloric festivals and events are particularly important. In addition, the city is within easy reach of other cultural centres such as Bruges, Ghent, Antwerp and Tournai.

JANUARY

Salon de l'Automobile: Parc des Expositions, Heysel. Held in the first half of January on every second year. The Brussels Car Show.
Brussels International Film Festival: Palais des Congrès, 3 Coudenberg. Not quite Cannes, but one of the important stops on the circuit.

FEBRUARY

Horse-racing: The 'Mardi Gras' prize at Sterrebeek Hippodrome, February. Brussels' premier racing event.
Batibouw: Parc des Expositions, Heysel. The Ideal Homes exhibition.

MARCH

Salon des Vacances: Parc des Expositions, Heysel. The Holiday Show.
International Book Fair: Palais des Congrès.
Eurantica: Parc des Expositions, Heysel. The international antiques show

APRIL

Royal Greenhouses: In the last day of April or the start of May (fixed by the 'blooming' time), the Serre Royales de Laeken, spectacular greenhouses at the Royal Palace of Laeken are open for free public visits.

Celebrating Belgium's National Day

Brussels road-race medals

MAY

Royal Greenhouses: The festival continues – see under April.

Queen Elisabeth International Music Competition: Palais des Beaux-Arts, 23 Rue Ravenstein, tel: 507 8200. The competition alternates between singing, violin and piano and attracts some of the world's most promising young musicians and singers.

Jazz Rallye: Held during the last week of May, at cafés and other venues throughout the city. A grand fiesta of jazz.

JUNE

Drive-in Cinema: A two-month programme of films (June to August every year) staged in the square in front of the Cinquantenaire arch, which is transformed into a drive-in cinema specially for the festival. A small slice of Americana in a classic Brussels setting.

Running: The annual Brussels 20-kilometre road-race begins from the Cinquantenaire.

Waterloo: Every five years a special 're-enactment' of the Battle of Waterloo of 1815, in which Napoleon was defeated by Prussian and British forces, is staged on the nearest weekend to the battle's 18 June anniversary. At the most recent re-enactment, staged in 1995, some 5,000 'soldiers' attired in appropriately coloured uniforms 'refought' the battle in front of a crowd of 100,000 people.

JULY

Drive-in Cinema: See under June.

The Ommegang: In the first week of July, on two separate evenings, in the Grand'Place. This impressive historic procession commemorates the entry of Habsburg Emperor Charles V and his court into Brussels in 1549. The Grand'Place is transformed into a scene from Renaissance times, as emperor, lords and ladies, horsemen and foot soldiers, magicians, dancers and loyal peasants bring a page of history to life.

Carpet of Flowers in the Grand'Place

Music: Every Sunday in the Bois de la Cambre, from 11am–1pm, open-air classical music and jazz concerts.

Fair: From mid-July to mid-August, fairground attractions near the Gare du Midi, in the annual Kermesse de Bruxelles. This event may be moving to Bruparck.

Grand'Place: Classical music concerts, held in Brussels' main square.

Fireworks: 21 July. A grand display in honour of Belgium's National Day.

Royal Palace: From 21 July–end August, exceptional visits to the Royal Palace in the Place du Palais.

Giants at the Meiboom ritual (August)

AUGUST

Royal Palace: See under July.
Fair: See Under July.
Grand'Place: See Under July.
Music: Venues vary. Brosella International Folk and Jazz Festival.
Folklore: 9 August. The planting of the Meiboom tree followed by a folkloric ritual and procession in the Grand'Place.
Flowers: Every second August (92, 94 etc), on the weekend nearest to 15 August, two-thirds of a million begonias are brought together in an intricately designed, multicoloured Carpet of Flowers in the Grand'Place.

Athletics: One of Belgium's most prestigious events, the Ivo Van Damme Memorial, takes place at the end of August, in the Heysel Stadium.

SEPTEMBER / NOVEMBER

Europalia: Every two years, from September–December, one particular country's art, culture and traditions go on display in a series of concerts, exhibitions, performances, etc. These events take place throughout Belgium, but are centred in Brussels. In 1995, Turkey was the intended country, but this was cancelled.

Cycling: At the Bois de la Cambre, the Eddy Merckx Grand Prix in cycle-racing.
Running: The Brussels Marathon.
Music: Exceptional classical music programmes of the Festival of Flanders and the Festival of Wallonia.
Brueghel: Around the middle of the month, in the Rue Haute area, an appropriately Brueghelian celebration, with giant puppets and street festivities in honour of the great local artist.
Jazz: Taking place in November, at venues throughout the city, is the Audi International Jazz Festival, one of the major events on the international jazz circuit.

DECEMBER

Europalia: See under September.
Christmas: Before Christmas, there is a Christmas Market in the Grand'Place. In addition there are the Christmas illuminations, and the Nativity Scene and Christmas Tree, also in the Grand'Place.

Practical Information

By Air

Brussels National Airport is at Zaventem just 8 miles (13km) from the city. Sabena is the national carrier. Most major airlines serve Brussels or fly to nearby cities such as Amsterdam and Paris. A new terminal has been built to cope with a rapid increase in traffic.

There is a thrice-hourly rail service during most of the day from the airport station for the 20-minute journey, costing 80 francs, to Brussels' Gare du Nord and Gare Centrale. A taxi to the city centre costs around 1,000 francs. Most drivers are as honest as taxi drivers anywhere, but there are also *taxis noirs* operating illegally from the airport – check the small print before accepting any offer to save you waiting in the taxi queue.

By Rail

There are regular international services from London (by Eurostar), Paris (by TGV), Amsterdam, Cologne, Ostend and Zeebrugge, the latter two connecting with car-ferry or jetfoil services from Britain. In addition, there are daily services into Brussels from Copenhagen, Moscow, Basle and Rome, plus weekly car-trains, in summer, to the Gare de Schaerbeek, from the south of France and Spain.

By Road

Brussels, one of Western Europe's traffic hubs, has a superb motorway net-

Brussels' Central Station

work. The E19 comes in from Paris 193 miles (310km) to the south, and from Amsterdam 144 miles (232km) to the north; the E40 from the car ferry terminals at Ostend and Zeebrugge 71 miles (114 km) to the west, and from Cologne 142 miles (228km) to the east; the E411 from Luxembourg 137 miles (220km) to the southeast. The Channel Tunnel has improved connections with London.

By Sea

Ostend and Zeebrugge are Belgium's two car-ferry terminals (Ostend also for the jetfoil), which connect with the British ports of Dover, Harwich and Hull (to Zeebrugge only). It's also possible to travel to Calais or Vlissingen and then by motorway to Brussels.

TRAVEL ESSENTIALS

When to Visit

The best time to come to Brussels is between April and October: the weather is better then and the museums and other attractions are open longer. Another good time to visit is July, when half the population disappears on their annual vacation and Brussels is at its most pleasant. Autumn is also an attractive month, particularly if you want to take the excursion to Spa (featured on *page 62* in this guide). The autumn colours are spectacular in the heavily-wooded Ardennes.

Visas and Passports

Citizens of the European Union and some other European countries do not need a passport but they must have an ID card (and in practice it still makes sense to carry a passport). Citizens of the EU, most other European countries, the USA, Australia, Canada, Japan and some other countries, do not need a visa. If in doubt, check with the Belgian consulate in your country of origin, or with your travel agent or air carrier.

Customs

There are no currency limitations, incoming or outgoing. Unpreserved meat products are not permitted; other unpreserved foodstuffs must be declared. Goods not incurring customs duties **EU** In principle there are no limits on goods on which duty has already been paid, but travellers may need to prove that excessive amounts are for personal use only. **Non-EU** 200 cigarettes or 50 cigars or 250g tobacco; 2 litres still wine; 1 litre spirits or 2 litres sparkling or fortified wine; 50g perfume and 0.25 litres eau de toilette.

Weather

The weather in July and August can be hot and humid, but Brussels is close to the North Sea and rain is not exactly rare even then. Generally, the climate is temperate. Winters are usually mild, with periods of snow. It rarely freezes enough to bring skaters out onto park ponds. Average summer temperature is 16°Celsius (61°F; in winter, 3°Celsius (37°F).

Clothing

A sweater or cardigan is a wise investment, even in summer, because evenings may be cool. An umbrella a vital accessory at almost any time. Warm clothes are needed in winter.

In most situations, whether for the opera, dinner or visiting, casual clothes are quite acceptable. Business style is formal and the absence of a tie will be frowned upon.

Electricity

The unit of electricity in Belgium is 220 volts AC.

Time

Belgium is on Central European Standard Time, with Daylight Saving Time a factor from late March to late September. This is GMT (UST) plus one hour in winter and plus two hours in summer. Most of the year Belgium time is one hour ahead of UK time.

GETTING ACQUAINTED

Geography

Brussels can be likened to a shallow bowl. The old heart of the city is the 'lower city', including the Grand'Place. The 'upper city', is the area east of the Grand'Place, around Avenue Louise. But as the city has steadily expanded, it has spread over the low hills in all directions.

Government and Economy

Brussels Capital Region is one of the three regions of the Belgian federal state. Only one of its 19 'communes' is actually called Brussels. 'Brussels' 'Bruxelles' in French, 'Brussel' in Dutch). The city is headquarters of the European Union and one of the seats of the European Parliament. It is also headquarters of the North Atlantic Treaty Organization (NATO).

Religion

Belgium is a Catholic country, although nowadays religion is honoured more in the breach than in the observance. Brussels, as a big city, tends to be ahead in that respect.

How Not to Offend

You can steal a Bruxellois' wife (or husband) but don't try to deprive them of their priority in traffic, *priorité de droite*; the result is sure to be bent bodywork and broken glass at the very least. Otherwise, you should manage fine. Bruxellois are very trustworthy.

Population

About 1 million, more than a quarter of whom are foreigners. Many of these are in Brussels as a result of the international institutions located in the city and multinational corporations which base their operations here. In recent years, a substantial Moslem community originating in North Africa and Turkey has developed.

MONEY MATTERS

Currrency

The unit of currency is the franc. Belgian francs (BF) have a different value from French and Swiss, but the same as those of Luxembourg. Notes come in denominations of 5,000, 1,000, 500 and 100 francs; coins in 50, 20, 5, and 1 francs, plus 50 centimes.

Credit Cards and Cheques

All the main international credit and charge cards are accepted. Traveller's cheques are better exchanged for francs at banks. If lost or stolen, traveller's cheques can be replaced; in the case of American Express usually within 24 hours. Eurocheques can be written to a value of BF7,000 if you have a Eurocheque card to back them up.

Cash Machines

There are automatic teller machines with names like 'Bancontact' and 'Mister Cash' all over the city. Many can be accessed by foreign Eurocheque and credit card holders, some also by the major charge-card holders.

Tipping

Taxis, most restaurants, hairdressers, etc very considerately include your tip in the bill, in the certainty that you couldn't fail to be impressed by the service. Ushers at some cinemas and theatres expect 20 francs for taking your ticket, while toilet attendants will make your visit a misery if you try to get past their saucer without leaving about 10 francs.

Taxes

Belgium appears dedicated to the proposition that all men are created equally liable to punitive taxation. However, there are shops, particularly in the main and upmarket shopping areas, that operate a tax-refund system for non-EU foreign visitors.

Money Changers

What some of the street establishments call 'commission' may leave you feeling you have been mugged. The exchanges at banks and the main railway stations are usually the least unreasonable. Anywhere else, be sure to ask questions about rates and commission charged.

GETTING AROUND

On Foot

The itineraries in this book are designed for walking, in conjunction with public transport. Brussels' centre is small enough that this is easily practical, although busy traffic can make it tiring.

A word of warning: Be careful at all times in traffic, especially where children might be crossing the road. Belgian road accident statistics are among the worst in Europe and many drivers prefer speed and bloody-mindedness to consideration. Black-and-white pedestrian crossings can be especially dangerous.

Taxis

They can be waved-down in the street but won't always stop. It's usually better to call one or wait at one of the many taxi ranks. Among the operators are **Taxis Verts**, tel: 349 4949; **Taxis Bleus**, tel: 268 0000; **Taxis Orange**, tel: 513 6200. Fares within Brussels are quite reasonable, starting at BF75 and going up by BF3 per kilometre.

Public Transport

The excellent metropolitan public transport network, operated by STIB, offers tickets at BF50 for a single journey; BF230 for a 5-journey card bought from the driver; BF310 for 10-journey card bought from an STIB or rail station; and BF125 for a one day card, which can be used as often as desired on bus, tram or metro line within the city (as with all prices, allow for 5-10 percent annual inflation). The 5- and 10-journey tickets must be cancelled in a platform or on-board machine, and re-entered on any connecting vehicle, each cancellation being valid for travel by one person on the bus, tram and metro network within a 1-hour period.

Train/Metro

There is a fast, modern and efficient metro service consisting of two main lines – 1 and 2 – which each split into two lines – 1A and 1B; 2A and 2B – outside the centre. Many metro

stations contain murals, paintings or sculptures by distinguished Belgian artists. The above-ground train service is also good, but not so handy within the city limits.

Bus/Tram

What applies to the metro applies also to these services, although buses in particular can be reduced to near-immobility in rush-hour. The tram is usually the fastest way to travel.

Car

Travelling by car in the city from 8am–7pm, Monday–Saturday (except maybe in July), tends to be nasty, brutish and long. If you bring a car, you would do well not to use it for sightseeing. All the usual international car-hire companies, plus some home-grown ones (try **Rent-A-Car**, 263 Avenue de la Couronne, tel: 649 8282), have offices in Brussels. Trams and buses always have traffic priority, as, usually, do vehicles coming from the right, unless the road is posted with orange diamond signs.

HOURS & HOLIDAYS

Business Hours

Shops are usually open Monday to Saturday 10am–6pm, although some of them close all day Monday. There are few late-night shops, but the neighbourhood 'corner store' may stay open until 9pm.

Banks are open 9am–4pm or 5pm, with an hour for lunch. On Friday, department stores and many other shops stay open until 9pm.

Public Holidays

New Year:	1 January
Easter Monday	
Labour Day:	1 May
Ascension Day:	6th Thursday after Easter
Whit Monday:	7th Monday after Easter
National Day:	21 July
Assumption:	15 August
All Saints:	1 November
Armistice:	11 November
Christmas:	25 December

Market Days

Grand'Place: Flowers, daily 8am–6pm, except Monday; Birds, Sunday 7am–2pm.
Place du Jeu de Balle: Flea market, daily 7am–2pm.
Place du Grand Sablon: Art and antiques, Saturday 9am–6pm, Sunday 9am–2pm.
Place de l'Agora: Crafts, weekend and public holiday, 10am–6pm.

Accommodation

Hotels

As a business centre, Brussels plays host to most of the international hotel groups. Too many hotels are now being built, and demand is often slack, meaning rates are often much lower than posted. Ask about reduced rates at weekends.

Price categories (for a double room): £=£20–£50; ££=£50–£100; £££=£100–£150; ££££=over £150.

Sas Royal Hotel
47 Rue du Fossé-aux-Loups
Tel: 219 2828
One of the city centre's luxury hotels, the SAS has won a reputation for good service, and a devoted following among residents of Brussels, thanks to its American-style cocktail bar, Henry J Bean's. ££££.

Carrefour De L'Europe
110 Rue du Marché-aux-Herbes
Tel: 504 9400
With possibly the best of all city-cen-

tre locations, facing the Place de l'Agora, and as flagship of Belgium's top-rated Sodehotel group, this new hotel should do all right. Its architecture harmonises with the Flemish Renaissance surroundings. *££££*.

STANHOPE HOTEL
9 Rue du Commerce
Tel: 506 9111
Three former townhouses converted to a hotel just off the stylish uptown shopping district of Avenue Louise and Porte de Namur, the Stanhope has all the grace of an English country hotel combined with an ideal city location. *££££*.

PULLMAN ASTORIA
103 Rue Royale
Tel: 217 6290
This is one of Brussels' gems. The Pullman Astoria opened its doors in 1909 under the name Astoria and was later taken over by Wagons-Lits. The railway link continues today in its Pullman Bar, styled after the famed Golden Arrow train, while its *belle epoque* lineage is perfectly reflected in the dazzling foyer and restaurant Le Palais Royal. *£££*.

AMIGO
1–3 Rue de l'Amigo
Tel: 547 4747
Just off the Grand'Place, it deserves its high reputation. *£££*.

CHATEAU DU LAC
87 Avenue du Lac
Tel: 654 1122
Located on the shore of Lac de Genval outside Brussels, the Château dates from the 1890s and is a copy of an old turreted abbey. Genval is popular for walks and the Château is one of its highlights. *£££*.

METROPOLE
31 Place de Brouckère
Tel: 217 2300
The Metropole's sumptuous French Renaissance splendour defies description. The hotel is simply unforgettable, with all the endangered style and grace that was Brussels' pre-Eurocity inheritance. What's more, it comes at a surprisingly moderate price. Recommended *££*.

EUROVILLAGE BRUSSELS
80 Boulevard Charlemagne
Tel: 230 8555
Ideally located for the Common Market, this hotel also has the reputation for being a good option for families. You may question the wisdom of exposing innocent children to the language and behaviour of practising Eurocrats, but perhaps they'll survive if you let them play in the garden. *££*.

MANOS
100–104 Chaussée de Charleroi
Tel: 539 3655
A mansion-style hotel in the area of Avenue Louise, Manos offers a different, more personal experience from the chain and business-oriented hotels. *££*.

New Hotel Siru
1 Place Rogier
Tel: 203 3580
Despite its unpromising location in the middle of a seedy (but gradually being demolished) red-light area, the Siru is Brussels' most surprising hotel. More than 100 Belgian artists were invited to 'decorate' each otherwise sparely furnished room with a painting, mural or sculpture on the theme of travel. *££.*

Kasteel Gravenhof
676 Alsembergsesteenweg, 1653 Dworp.
Tel: 380 4499
Maybe the nearest thing Brussels has to a Spanish *parador*, Gravenhof is an old Flemish-style château located not far from Brussels. If you feel as to the manor born, perhaps this is the place for you. *££.*

Queen Anne
110 Boulevard Emile Jacqmain
Tel: 217 1600
In an area of Brussels that may be looking up after years of steady decline. The rooms are business-traveller orientated and the location is just enough off the main centre to be not totally convenient, but in compensation it's fairly quiet. *£.*

Welcome
5 Rue du Peuplier
Tel: 219 9546
A little wonder, only six rooms, with four more more on the way. Its young entrepreneur owner fusses proudly around both it and the associated La Truite d'Argent restaurant on the Marché des Poissons, where the fishing boats once docked. *£.*

Sabina
78 Rue du Nord
Tel: 218 2637
Converted town house from the 1920s in a quiet street near the inner ring road and a 10- to 15-minute walk from the centre. *£.*

Les Bluets
124 Rue Berckmans
Tel: 534 3983
A beautiful building from 1864. The enthusiastic proprietress will point out the finer details of her old family hotel at the drop of a question. Located in a quiet, characterful street near Avenue Louise. *£.*

Youth Hostels

Auberge de Jeunesse Jacques Brel
30 Rue de la Sablonnière
Tel: 218 0187
This Youth Hostel also includes facilities for disabled people.

Auberge de Jeunesse Bruegel
2 Rue du Saint-Esprit
Tel: 511 0436

Centre d'Hébergement de l'Agglomération Bruxelloise
8 Rue Traversière
Tel: 217 0158

Sleep-Well
27 Rue de la Blanchisserie
Tel: 218 5050

Auberge de Jeunesse Jean Nihon
4 Rue de l'Eléphant
Tel: 410 3858

Staying With Local Families

For further information on this, and also for au pair positions, contact:

New Windrose
21A Avenue Dejaer
Tel: 534 7191

Camping

There are no camping sites in Brussels itself, but there are several within easy reach of the city:

CAMPING PAUL CHARLES
114 Avenue Albert 1er, 1332 Genval.
Tel: 653 6215

CAMPING VELDKANT
64 Veldkantstraat, 1850 Grimberge.
Tel: 269 2597

CAMPING WELCOME
104 Kouterstraat, 3090 Overijse
Tel: 687 7577

CAMPING DE RENIPONT
7A Rue du Ry Beau Ry, 1380 Ohain
(near Waterloo)
Tel: 654 0670

HEALTH & EMERGENCIES
Pharmacies
A list of out-of-hours (duty) pharmacies is posted on the front of every pharmacy. Duty pharmacies change every week.

Medical/Dental Services
Emergency telephone numbers: *Accidents* 100
Standby doctors: 24 hours a day, tel: 479 1818 or 242 4344
Standby dentists: Monday to Saturday 9pm–7am, and Saturday 7am–Monday 7am, tel: 426 1026 or 428 5888. Anti-Poison Centre (for emergency advice), tel: 345 4545

Crime/Trouble
Although crime does exist – in the main petty theft from cars and of handbags and wallets – it is not really something to worry about. Violent crime, muggings and assault are unlikely to be encountered. Anyone who comes from a big city where violent crime has become part of everyday life will probably be favourably impressed by Brussels.

Lost Property
Aircraft: Brussels National Airport arrivals hall, tel: 723 6011
Airport: Brussels National Airport visitors hall, tel: 722 3940, weekdays only
Train: Gare du Nord, tel: 224 6112, 7.30am–5.30pm
Metro, Bus, Tram: 15 Avenue de la Toison d'Or, tel: 515 2394, 9.30am–12.30pm

Police
Emergency telephone numbers *Police* and *Gendarmerie* 101; *Fire* 100

COMUNICATIONS
Post
Normal post office hours are Monday–Friday 9am–5pm. Some offices are open on Friday evening and Saturday morning. The office at **Gare du Midi** is open every day, 24 hours a day. Letters and postcards, up to 20 grams, to EU countries cost BF16; to other countries BF30. Maximum permitted weight for letters is 2 kilograms.

Telephone
The country code for Belgium is 32. Coins of BF5 and BF20 are accepted by public telephone; 'telecards' cost BF200 and BF500. To call other countries first dial the international access code 00, then the country code: Australia (61); France (33); Italy (39); Netherlands (31); Spain (34); US and Canada (1).

To use a US credit phone card, call the company's access number below: AT&T, tel: 11-0010; MCI, tel: 078 11-0012; Sprint, tel 078 11-0014.

MEDIA

A weekly English-language magazine, *The Bulletin*, circulates. The *International Herald Tribune* and British and Irish newspapers are widely available, but not English-language papers of other countries. Cable television offers British and American networks, including the BBC and CNN. BBC Radio 4 can be picked up with near-perfect reception as can the BBC World Service and Voice of America.

USEFUL INFORMATION

For the Disabled

Services for disabled people are as good, or bad, as in most West European countries. Museums and other public buildings usually have special access for wheelchairs; not so public transport, although metro stations are better in this respect. There is a limited number of reserved parking spaces for disabled drivers.

For Children

Some itineraries should interest children, eg Mini-Europe and the Océade at Bruparck, the Battle of Waterloo, boating in the Bois de la Cambre, the Africa Museum, Autoworld, etc. Here are some other possibilities:

Baby sitters: Students from the Université Libre de Bruxelles jobs centre, tel: 650 2171.
Children's farms: *Ferme du Parc Maximilien*, 21 Quai du Batelage, tel: 217 6592; *Jardin Botanique de Jette*, 172 Petite Rue Sainte-Anne, tel: 479 8053; *Ferme Modèle d'Uccle*, 93 Vieille Rue du Moulin, tel: 374 1896.

Leisure Centre: *Walibi Theme and Adventure Park*, and its associated aquatic theme-park *Aqualibi*, at Wavre, 12½ miles (20km) from Brussels. By train from Brussels Nord, Centrale or Midi, line Ottignies/Louvain-la-Neuve, to Bierges station, tel: (010) 414466.
Museums: *Children's Museum*, 15 Rue du Bourgmestre, tel: 640 0107, open Wednesday, weekend and school holiday 2.30pm–5.30pm; *Toy Museum*, 24 Rue de l'Association, tel: 219 6168, open 10am–6pm.

Bookshops

W H Smith, 71 Boulevard Adolphe Max, tel: 219 2708.

Museums

Many of the city's museums are listed in the various itineraries. Some others are:

MUSEE DU COSTUME ET DE LA DENTELLE
6 Rue de la Violette
Tel: 512 7709
Costumes and lace museum. Open Tuesday, Thursday, Friday 10am–12.30pm, 1.30–5pm, October to March until 4pm; weekends 2–4.30pm; closed Monday and Wednesday.

MAISON ERASME
31 Rue du Chapitre
Tel: 521 1383
This is the house where the philosopher Erasmus lived in 1521. Open 10am–noon and 2–5pm, closed Tuesday and Friday.

MUSEE DU FORET DE SOIGNES
6 Duboislaan, Hoeilaart
Tel: 657 2203
Flora and fauna of the forest; free guided visits on request. Open May, June, September, October 1.30–5.30pm.

MUSEE DE LA GUEUZE
56 Rue Gheude, Anderlecht
Tel: 520 2891, 521 4928
Gueuze is Brussels' best-known beer. Monday to Friday 8.30am–4.30pm, Saturday January to May and 15 October to 31 December 10am–6pm, 1 June to 14 October 9.30am–1pm.

MUSEE HORTA
25 Rue Américaine, Saint-Gilles
Tel: 537 1692
The home of the renowned *art nouveau* architect Victor Horta. Open 2–5.30pm, closed Monday.

MUSEE NATIONAL DE LA RESISTANCE
14 Rue Van Lint, Anderlecht
Tel: 522 4041, 520 6040
Documents the secret world of the Resistance during two World Wars. Open Monday, Tuesday and Thursday 9am–noon, 1–4pm.

LANGUAGE

There are three official languages in Belgium: French, Dutch and German. However, Brussels is officially bilingual – French and Dutch – with street names always given in both, eg: **Avenue Louise/Louizalaan**. English is widely spoken.

SPORT

Keeping fit is not a major priority in Brussels, although with so much good food around the need surely exists. Like everything else, however, this is changing and more fitness centres are opening.

Fitness Centres
American Gym, 144 Boulevard Général Jacques, tel: 640 5992
California Gym, 298 Chaussée d'Ixelles, tel: 640 9344
European Athletic City, 25A Avenue Winston Churchill, tel: 345 3077

Bowling
Information from the Fédération Sportive de Bowling, 550 Chaussée de Louvain, 1030 Brussels, tel: 732 4808. Some bowling alleys:

Bowling Crosly Brunswick, 43 Quai au Foin, tel: 217 2801
Bowling Crosly Empereur, 36 Boulevard de l'Empereur, tel: 512 0874

Golf
Information on the numerous courses in and around Brussels from the Fédération Royale Belge de Golf, 110 Chaussée de la Hulpe, 1170 Brussels, tel: 672 2389.

Riding
There are many stables in the Brussels area and information can be obtained from the Fédération Royale Belge des Sports Equestres, 156 Avenue Houba de Strooper, 1020 Brussels, tel: 478 5056. A few stables:
L'Etrier, 19 Champ du Vert Chasseur, tel: 374 2860 or 3870.
Tervuren Horse Club, 121 Steenweg op Duisburg, Tervuren, tel: 767 6402.
Centre Equestre de la Cambre, 872 Chaussée de Waterloo, tel: 375 3408.

Tennis

Information on tennis facilities is available from the Fédération Royale Belge de Tennis, 203 Galesie Porte de Louise, tel: 513 2927.

Swimming

Information from the Fédération Royale Belge de Natation, 28 Rue Chevreuil, tel: 513 8708.
A few pools:
Poseidon, 2 Avenue des Vaillants, tel: 771 6655. Daily 8am–7pm.
Calypso, 60 Avenue L Wiener, tel: 673 3929. Daily 8am–6pm.

Marché-aux-Herbes, tel: 504 0390. Monday to Saturday (January to May and October to December) 9am–6pm, (June to September) 9am–7pm; Sunday (January to March and November to December) 1–5pm, (April, May, October) 9am–6pm (June to September) 9am–7pm.

City Tours

Chatterbus (for individual–and individualistic–guides): 12 Rue des Thuyas, tel: 673 1835.
De Boeck's: 8 Rue de la Colline, tel: 513 7744.
ARAU (for non-mainstream architecture and history): 2 Rue du Midi, tel: 513 4761.

Business

Ministry of Economic Affairs, 23 Square de Meeûs, 1040 Brussels, tel: 506 5111; fax: 514 0635.
Brussels Chamber of Commerce, 500 Avenue Louise, 1050 Brussels, tel: 648 5002; fax: 640 9328.
Brussels International Trade Mart, Atomium Square, 1020 Brussels, tel: 478 4989; fax: 478 6258.
American Chamber of Commerce, 5 Avenue des Arts, 1040 Brussels, tel: 513 6770; fax: 513 7928.
British Chamber of Commerce, 15 Rue d'Egmont, 1050 Brussels, tel: 540 9030, fax: 512 8363.

USEFUL ADRESSES

Tourist Offices

The two main city-centre offices are extremely helpful.
Tourist Information Brussels, Town Hall (Hôtel de Ville), Grand'Place, tel: 513 8940. Monday to Saturday 9am–6pm; Sunday (in summer) 9am–6pm, (in winter) 10am–2pm, closed (on Sunday) 1 December to 28 February.
Belgian Tourist Office, 61 Rue du

FURTHER READING

Insight Guide: Brussels and *Insight Guide: Belgium*. Companion to this book, from Apa Publications' award-winning series. Also available *Insight: Compact Guide Brussels*, a mini-encyclopaedia.
Guide Delta Bruxelles. Lists almost 1,700 restaurants.
The Great Beers of Belgium. By Michael Jackson, the world authority on the subject.

Art & Photo Credits

All photography except where otherwise stated **Alex Kouprianoff**
75, 77, 81 **George Taylor**
Cartography **Berndtson & Berndtson**